Muriel Spark

Twayne's English Authors Series

Kinley E. Roby, Editor
Northeastern University

TEAS 460

MURIEL SPARK
(1918–   )
Photograph by Jerry Bauer

Muriel Spark

By Dorothea Walker

Nassau Community College,
State University of New York

Twayne Publishers
A Division of G.K. Hall & Co. • *Boston*

To Cory and Erin,
angels in a fallen world

Muriel Spark

Dorothea Walker

Copyright 1988 by G.K. Hall & Co.
All rights reserved.
Published by Twayne Publishers
A Division of G.K. Hall & Co.
70 Lincoln Street
Boston, Massachusetts 02111

Copyediting supervised by Lewis DeSimone
Book production by Janet Zietowski
Book design by Barbara Anderson

Typeset in 11 pt. Garamond
by Williams Press, Inc., Albany, New York

Printed on permanent/durable acid-free paper
and bound in the United States of America

Library of Congress Cataloging in Publication Data

Walker, Dorothea.
  Muriel Spark / by Dorothea Walker.
  p.   cm.—(Twayne's English authors series ; TEAS 460)
  Bibliography: p. 114
  Includes index.
  ISBN 0-8057-6960-9 (alk. paper)
  1. Spark, Muriel—Criticism and interpretation.   I. Title.
II. Series.
PR6037.P29Z96   1988
823'.914—dc19   87-20140
                                                              CIP

Contents

120499

About the Author

Dorothea Walker is a professor of English at Nassau Community College, State University of New York, where she teaches courses in women's studies, literature, and writing. She holds an A.B. degree from Hunter College, City University of New York, and M.A. and Ph.D. degrees from St. John's University, Hillcrest, New York.

Professor Walker has published a book on Alice Brown, a New England writer, in Twayne's United States Authors Series; and a book on Sheila Kaye-Smith in Twayne's English Authors Series. She has also published articles and book reviews in women's studies and American literature.

Professor Walker is active in affirmative action. She developed the first women's studies course in the English department of her college. Active in women's organizations, she works constantly toward the attainment of full equality for women.

Preface

When Derek Stanford, a friend of Muriel Spark's and an admirer of her work, wrote in 1963 that there had been little written on her up to that time but that without doubt much would be written, he showed himself a prophet. In the years that have passed since the time he published his biographical and critical study of Muriel Spark, much indeed has been written about her: reviews, articles, doctoral dissertations, and books. The wealth of scholarship generated by her work since the publication of her first novel, *The Comforters* (1957), until the publication of her latest, *The Only Problem* (1984), reveals the tremendous interest generated by her work. I have drawn on this scholarship to help the reader of her novels to a better understanding of them.

That Muriel Spark is a celebrated writer is attested by the abundance of critical comment as well as by her popular success. Each new novel is a literary event. The wit and humor of her characters, who reveal the problem of living in a God-created world without being orthodox Christians, give the reader an enjoyable reading experience. But the general (and even the scholarly) reader may have difficulty in understanding the underlying vision upon which the plot builds and the characters act.

For this reason, I have analyzed what I consider to be Muriel Spark's most important novels from the standpoint of this vision. I have given the general reader insights into the author's themes and some understanding of the way in which she reveals them. I have occasionally referred the reader to important or interesting criticism on aspects of the novels other than those I have chosen to discuss, as well as to commentary that further explains my own ideas. I have analyzed the novels in chronological order, except where exigencies such as similarity of theme required a departure.

Muriel Spark's talent is unique. She sees Roman Catholicism, the religion she came to embrace, as underlying all truth and as the revealer of that truth. For her, the world is God's. But it is a fallen world, unredeemed in its inability to achieve God's plan for it, although some members of humanity, in her view, manage to lift themselves up in partial redemption. Even though she has been compared in moral vision to Flannery O'Connor, Evelyn Waugh, and Graham Greene, the satire and wit used to image this moral vision are distinctly hers. Her mythical, comic-tragic, and religious emphasis may seem like that of William Golding, Samuel Beckett, Iris Murdoch, or Malcolm Lowry; yet her uniqueness is apparent in the individual novels. She has been compared to Isaac Bashevis Singer in her treatment of the supernatural; yet the use she makes of it is completely different. Her *Mandelbaum Gate* has even been compared to E. M. Forster's *Passage to India* despite the obvious differences.

She is not a "Catholic" novelist in the sense of Waugh and Greene (although they both argue that they are novelists who happen to be Catholics). For the most part, her Catholicism fails to embrace ordinary Catholics, and some of her most satiric portraits are of born Catholics. It has been remarked that no one would be tempted to become a Catholic from reading her novels. Finally, the realism concerning sex and sordid elements in life, so prominent in novels after World War II, does not appear in her portraits. But in intricacy of plot, wit of dialogue, and inventiveness of character, Muriel Spark remains a gifted novelist who shows in each novel an innate originality. She cannot be categorized.

A recent review of her latest novel, *The Only Problem,* in the *Times Literary Supplement* indicates that Muriel Spark is easy to read and hard to talk about. The necessity of accepting her penchant for preternatural or supernatural elements, of following characters who come and go in the fashion of a soap opera, and of attempting to understand her considerable use of witty satire—all combine to place extraordinary demands upon the reader who wishes to gain some insight into her view of the world rather than to settle for simply enjoying the story. To this end I have analyzed the novels with the intention of showing the scope of a remarkable imagination combined with an extraordinary talent.

It is my wish that the reader will gain a knowledge of Muriel Spark that encompasses the relationship of her life to her work as well as an understanding of the value of that work to our literary heritage.

I wish to express my appreciation to Professor Edith Forbes and Professor Vera Jerwick, reference librarians at Nassau Community College, for their never-failing help in obtaining critical material and their expert assistance in searching out hard-to-find facts. I would like to thank Mr. Milton Camirand, research librarian at the *Long Island Catholic* for his success in securing a copy of the encyclical "Dominum et Vivificantem" (The Lord and Giver of Life); Mrs. Dorothy Olding of Harold Ober Associates (Spark's agent) for her prompt and courteous answers to my inquiries; and in memoriam, Mrs. Eileen Staaz, my kind neighbor, for her friendship and encouragement during periods of frustration. I wish also to thank Professor Kinley E. Roby of Northeastern University for his excellent editing.

I must express my special gratitude to Professor Paul A. Doyle of Nassau Community College, not only for his suggestion that this book be written, but for his invaluable aid in pointing out weaknesses in the first draft and for reading the work in final manuscript form. Above all, I thank him for his encouragement when the task seemed overwhelming. Without his confidence in my ability, the book would not have been written.

Dorothea Walker

Nassau Community College,
State University of New York

Acknowledgments

I wish to express my gratitude to the following for permission to quote from copyrighted material:

To Harper & Row for permission to quote from *The Prime of Miss Jean Brodie:* specified selection from *The Prime of Miss Jean Brodie* by Muriel Spark. Copyright © 1961 by Muriel Spark. Reprinted by permission of Harper & Row, Publishers, Inc.

To St. Martin's Press, Inc. for permission to quote from *The Faith and Fiction of Muriel Spark* by Ruth Whittaker.

To Harold Ober Associates for permission to quote from the following:
The Comforters. Copyright © 1957 by Copyright Administration Limited. Copyright renewed 1985 by Copyright Administration Limited.
The Bachelors. Copyright © 1960 by Copyright Administration Limited.
Memento Mori. Copyright © 1959 by Copyright Administration Limited.
The Ballad of Peckham Rye. Copyright © 1960 by Copyright Administration Limited.
The Mandelbaum Gate. Copyright © 1965 by Copyright Administration Limited.
The Abbess of Crewe. Copyright © 1974 by Copyright Administration Limited.
Territorial Rights. Copyright © 1979 by Copyright Administration Limited.
Loitering with Intent. Copyright © 1981 by Copyright Administration Limited.
The Takeover. Copyright © 1976 by Copyright Administration Limited.
The Driver's Seat. Copyright © 1970 by Copyright Administration Limited.
The Only Problem. Copyright © 1984 by Copyright Administration Limited.

Chronology

1918   Muriel Sarah Spark born 1 February in Edinburgh, Scotland, daughter of Bernard (an engineer) and Sarah Elizabeth (Uezzell) Camberg.

1924–1936   Attends James Gillespie's School in Edinburgh.

1937   Marries S. O. Spark in Rhodesia. Robin (son) born.

1938   Divorced from S. O. Spark.

1944   Returns to England. Writes news items for political intelligence department of British government. Affiliated with *Argentor* (jewelry trade magazine).

1945   Founds *Forum* (literary magazine). Works as commercial press agent.

1947   Becomes editor of *Poetry Review* and a member of the Royal Society of Literature.

1949   Named fellow in Royal Society of Literature; General Secretary, Poetry Society; Honorary member, PEN, American Academy and Institute of Arts and Letters. "Elegy in a Kensington Churchyard."

1950   Becomes Review Editor, *European Affairs. Tribute to Wordsworth* (editor and author of introduction with Derek Stanford).

1951   Receives *Observer* short story prize for "The Seraph and the Zambesi." *Child of Light: A Reassessment of Mary Wollstonecraft Shelley.*

1952   *The Fanfarlo and Other Verses. A Selection of Poems by Emily Brontë* (editor and author of introduction).

1953   Baptized into Anglican church by Reverend C. O. Rhodes. *Emily Brontë: Her Life and Work* (with Derek Stanford). *My Best Mary: The Letters of Mary Shelley* (with Derek Stanford). *John Masefield.* Begins reading, with Derek Stanford, the works of John Henry Newman.

1954 Received into the Roman Catholic church by Father Philip Caraman. *The Letters of the Brontës: A Selection* (editor). Receives advance from Macmillan for a novel. Begins living in "St. Jude's Cottage," owned by the Carmelites on their grounds at Aylesfore.

1957 *The Comforters. Letters of John Henry Newman* (with Derek Stanford).

1958 *Robinson. The Go-Away Bird and Other Stories.*

1959 *Memento Mori.*

1960 *The Bachelors. The Ballad of Peckham Rye. The Seraph and the Zambesi.*

1961 Spends two months in Israel. *The Prime of Miss Jean Brodie. Voices at Play* (short stories and radio plays).

1962–1966 Moves to New York City. Works in office supplied to her by the *New Yorker* magazine, to which she is a contributor.

1963 *The Girls of Slender Means. Doctors of Philosophy* (a play produced in London in 1962).

1965 *The Mandelbaum Gate.* Receives *Yorkshire Post* book-of-the-year award for *The Mendelbaum Gate.*

1966 Moves to Italy. Receives James Tait Black Memorial Prize for *The Mendelbaum Gate. The Brontë Letters: Selected and with an Introduction by Muriel Spark* (New Edition).

1967 *Collected Poems I. Collected Stories I.* Named Commander, Order of the British Empire.

1968 *The Public Image. The Very Fine Clock* (juvenile).

1970 *The Driver's Seat.*

1971 *Not to Disturb.* Receives LL.D., University of Strathclyde.

1973 *The Hothouse by the East River.*

1974 *The Abbess of Crewe.*

1976 *The Takeover.*

1979 *Territorial Rights.*

1981   *Loitering with Intent.* Receives Booker McConnell Prize nomination for *Loitering with Intent.*

1982   *Bang-Bang-You're Dead and Other Stories.*

1984   *The Only Problem.*

1985   *The Stories of Muriel Spark.*

Chapter One
Early Life and Influences

Muriel Sarah Spark was born in Edinburgh, Scotland, on 1 February 1918. Her father, Bernard Camberg, was Jewish, and her mother, Sarah Uezzell Camberg, English. The school she attended, James Gillespie's School in Edinburgh, was one of Scotland's great endowed schools. She studied the Old Testament thoroughly and of her other reading she later said she most enjoyed the reasonableness and clarity of the prose of John Stuart Mill. The background of her best-known novel, *The Prime of Miss Jean Brodie,* takes its Presbyterism atmosphere from this school.

Spark says she was "the school's Poet and Dreamer."[1] Although she considered herself primarily a poet, she also kept a diary. Further, she invented letters to herself from boyfriends, making sure that she left them where her mother would find them. "This strange activity seems like a bid for an emotional life of her own, constrained at the same time by a need to submit that life to control. It is indicative of her future craft as a novelist, the action of a plotter and a fiction-maker, creating situations analogous to those with real potential, but over which control can be exercised."[2]

She lived in Edinburgh until 1937, when she went to Rhodesia. There she married S. O. Spark. She had a son, Robin. She has not written a novel about this period in her life, but some of her best short stories are set in Africa.

Divorced from her husband in 1938, Muriel Spark lived in Africa and Rhodesia until 1944, when she returned to England.[3] She writes that she had "felt very strongly the lack of communication with the world to which [she] belonged. There was no advanced cultural life in Africa by which to measure all [she] experienced there," and she "longed throughout the early years of the war to get back to a place of books and ideas even though the bombs were falling."[4]

On her return to England, she took a job in the political intelligence department of the British Foreign Office and worked at Woburn Abbey, a large, stately English home, amid conditions of great secrecy. Derek Stanford, a fellow of the Royal Society of Literature and a close friend of hers (she dedicated her anthology *The Go-Away Bird and Other Stories* to him), in writing about his acquaintance with Spark at this time, recalls that the aim of the office for which she worked was to undermine the morale of the Nazis through specially slanted news articles. He recalls that "the best of the stories which Miss Spark and her colleagues broadcast for export was to the effect that Hitler's trousers had been burnt off him when the bomb exploded in the General's Revolt."[5] This story reveals an early example of Spark's comic cynicism, her earthiness, and her ability to focus on witty detail, a hallmark of her style.

After the war, Spark worked on a magazine dealing with jewels and precious metals called *Argentor*. This was a job that appealed to the exotic in her nature; it necessitated her spending much time in research on ornaments in London museums. Hearing that the Poetry Society was looking for a secretary, she obtained that position, soon rising to editor of the *Poetry Review*. As editor, she insisted that all published poems be paid for, a practice that particularly attracted young poets. But her aim remained to keep a balance between the traditional poem and the avant-garde. Her sympathetic portrayal of Percy Mannering, the old bard in *Memento Mori*, illustrates her affection for poets, traditional as well as avant-garde.[6]

When Spark left the editorship of the *Poetry Review*, she started a poetry magazine, *Forum*. At this time she was writing criticism as well as poetry, but her first volume of poems, *The Fanfarlo and Other Verses* was not published until 1952. She lived in Vicarage Gate, off Church Street, near the Anglican Church of Saint Mary Abbott's. The little graveyard at the back of this church dates from the eighteenth century. Sometimes she would sit in the graveyard writing a poem. Her "Elegy in a Kensington Churchyard" (1949) was suggested by the graveyard. Her novel *Loitering with Intent* begins, "One day in the middle of the twentieth century I sat in an old graveyard . . . in the Kensington area of London," and Fleur, heroine of the story, sits "on the stone slab of some Victorian grave" writing her poem.[7] Most of her novels contain similar autobiographical references.

In 1951 her very experimental story, "The Seraph and the Zambesi," won the *Observer* short story contest. This story encompasses Baudelaire's story "The Fanfarlo" and her own experience in South Africa. It is not the usual Christmas story, and many of the paper's readers wrote protesting the choice. But among the judges were Phillip Toynbee and Sir Harold Nicolson, and they were enthusiastic. The editor of the paper, David Astor, "was so keen about the story that he turned up about 2 A.M. on Sunday morning at the door of Miss Spark's flat, with the first copy of the paper, still wet with news-print, in his hand."[8]

According to Derek Stanford, it was about this time that Spark's imagination became attracted to the "magic universe of Catholic thought, with its infinite spaces inhabited by visible and invisible spirits." Cardinal Newman's remark that " 'a Christian view of the universe is necessarily a poetical one' . . . so took Miss Spark's fancy that she once copied out his words" in a book she gave to Derek. Stanford recalls that later, after she became a Catholic, she told him how the "Catholic image of the heavens seemed to her very much more economic. 'Otherwise all that space is wasted.' "[9]

These religious feelings led her to make a commitment to a formal religion. And her novels reveal that for her religion "is the central fact of existence."[10] From her schooldays until 1952, she had acknowledged no religious faith and called herself a "pagan," but by 1953 she was ready to be baptized into the Anglican church. The baptism was effected by the Reverend C. O. Rhodes, an ex-editor of the *Church of England Newspaper*, a controversial weekly. She attended the church where T. S. Eliot worshiped, Saint Stephen's, for a time. This was "high-Church," its ritual close to that of the Roman Catholic church. She attended her first mass in this church and was considerably impressed with it.

With Stanford, she had begun to read the writings of John Henry Newman. Stanford recalls that she was fascinated by Newman's style and personality as well as by the clarity and courtesy of his prose. He feels that "Newman's aloneness in his life (both as an Anglican and a Catholic) made her . . . feel some kind of identity with him. Like her, he had come first to High Anglicanism and then to Roman Catholicism."[11] For both Muriel Spark and Cardinal Newman, Catholicism seemed to be a religion that explained their own beliefs rather than one in which they had to adjust to a different intellectual view. Spark once said, "The reason I became a Roman Catholic was because it explained me," and in the same interview, she said she was a "Catholic Animal."[12]

But she did not go immediately from Anglicanism to Roman Catholicism. She attributes the delay to her dislike of Catholics. She says, "I was put off a long time by individual Catholics, living ones, I mean.

Good God, I used to think, if I become Catholic, will I grow like them?"[13] Catholics do not always fare well as characters in her novels.

But when she did start receiving instructions, it was from a Benedictine priest, Father Aegius, whose friendship dated back to the time she had published some of his poetry in the *Poetry Review*. While receiving instructions, she became ill, caused partly by undernourishment. In response Father Aegius would serve her biscuits and hot milk after each lesson. She was trying to write a work based on the Book of Job at the time, a subject she dealt with later (*The Only Problem*, her most recent novel, has as its theme the Book of Job). The experience she underwent appears vividly in her portrayal of Caroline in *The Comforters*. Caroline, also feeling the stress of conversion and authorship, receives similar nourishment from a priest friend. The spiritual instruction resulted in Muriel Spark's reception into the Catholic church in 1954 by her good friend Father Philip Caraman, editor of the *Month,* a Jesuit magazine.[14]

But undernourishment and the psychological stress caused by her conversion, added to a low income, resulted in nervous strain. She received financial aid from various people, including Graham Greene, whom she had never met. The economic assistance had been offered on the condition that she seek medical and psychological help. She gravitated to Jungian theory, seeing the unconscious imagery of the psyche as closely related to the artistic process. Years later, in a 1961 interview, she explains, "even if a particular character has struck my imagination, one person I've met, I never reproduce the character in the book. It's always my experience of hundreds of characters, and also a kind of memory that I can't explain, almost as if I remember the past before I was born."[15]

Apparently her conversion and the therapy she received after it worked as a liberating force, as six months later she was completely well and able to write her first full-length novel. Alan Maclean of the London firm of Macmillan invited her to write a novel for them. "Mr. Maclean, whose business it was to help give Macmillan a share of the 'new look,' picked on Miss Spark as a promising literary filly."[16]

With the Macmillan advance, Spark retired to a tiny cottage owned by the Carmelite friary at Aylesfore called "St. Jude's Cottage." Saint Jude, the patron saint of hopeless cases, did not in any way have to be called upon by the promising novelist, for the novel *The Comforters* was an immediate success upon its publication in 1957. Evelyn Waugh, a fellow convert, praised it in an address to the PEN Club and reviewed it at length in the *Spectator*. Overall the reviews were favorable. The novel has an underlying theme of Catholicism and depicts Catholics. Her close encounters with Catholics during her stay at Aylesfore apparently did not change her view of them, as her presentations in *The Comforters* are scarcely flattering, and her characterization of Mrs. Hogg is one of the most savage of any of the Catholics in her work. As a new convert, her complete acceptance of the tenets of Catholicism had the effect of producing an intolerance for those whose lives were lived under a less idealistic vision.

Spark's conversion to Roman Catholicism was the major influence of her career, turning her from poetry, short story, and critical writing to the novel. In 1961 she states, "I wasn't able to work and to do any of my writing until I became a Catholic."[17] In an article, "My Conversion," published in the autumn of 1961, she writes, "The Catholic belief is a norm from which one can depart. It's not a fluctuating thing. . . . Nobody can deny I speak with my own voice as a writer now, because I was never sure what I was, the ideas teemed, but I could never sort them out. I was talking and writing with other people's voices all the time. But not any longer."[18] Although brought up a Presbyterian, Spark feels that she had "no clear beliefs at all" until 1952, when she became "an Anglican, intellectually speaking."[19]

It is difficult to place Spark in the context of other contemporary English novelists. Malcolm Bradbury divides postwar English novels into two streams: one, the realistic "contemporary," uses middle-class or working-class characters in the new social atmosphere of postwar Britain favored by such writers as "Amis, Wain, Sillitoe, Braine and David Storey"; and the second includes more "fantastic" and "visionary" works by such figures as "Beckett, Malcolm Lowry, Durrell, Iris Murdoch, William Golding, Muriel Spark." Bradbury admits that this alignment is not quite accurate: some writers in the first group might show in some of their works attributes of the second group and vice versa. Then he places a "number of recognizably important . . . novelists . . . somehow between the two sets." These writers are Golding (*Lord of the Flies,* 1954), Nigil Dennis (*Cards of Identity,* 1955), Muriel Spark (*Memento Mori,* 1959), B. S. Johnson (*Travelling People,* 1963), and Doris Lessing (*The Habit of Loving,* 1957). In these writers he finds a "characteristically mythical, religious, or comic grotesque bias, a disposition towards a romance-like form, or . . . fantastic vigour . . . sustaining authority from, the experimental spirit."[20] The placing of Spark first in one group and then "between" the two groups emphasizes the difficulty of categorizing her. The accuracy of Bradbury's assessment and comparison of Spark's early novels is not denied. But Spark's talent ultimately defies categorization. This can be seen in the following analysis of her novels.

Chapter Two
Finding Identity as a Catholic and as a Novelist

The underlying themes of *The Comforters, Memento Mori, The Bachelors,* and *The Ballad of Peckham Rye* concern Spark's distrust of the novel as an art form and her uncertainty about her identity as a newly formed Roman Catholic. Frank Kermode, in analyzing her early work, points out that *The Comforters* "looks into the question of what kind of truth can be told in a novel." The "plot is deliberately complicated, since the question asked is, how can such an organized muddle of improbabilities, further disordered by the presumptuous claims of the writer on space and time, say anything true or interesting?"[1] Joan Leonard points out that for Spark fiction links heaven and earth, and it is religious in the sense that it brings the supernatural to light.[2] Yet Spark herself has said that she does not claim her novels are truth. In an interview broadcast over the British Broadcasting Company, she states: "I don't claim that my novels are true . . . I claim that they are fiction, out of which a kind of truth emerges. And I keep in mind that what I am writing is fiction, because I am interested in truth— absolute truth. . . . There is a metaphorical truth and moral truth, and what they call anagogical. . . . and there is absolute truth, in which I believe things which are difficult to believe, but I believe them because they are absolute."[3] Kermode points out that this "absolute truth is, of course, the teaching of the Roman Catholic Church. The lies of fiction can partake of truth, perhaps give it a useful, though imperfect human application. . . . Mrs. Spark is . . . concerned with the comedy of the situation. The novelist, presumptuous, arbitrary, scheming, and faking, lying like the fiend, makes things like worlds, plots absurdly like God's."[4]

The Comforters

The concern with truth branches into two distinct areas in *The Comforters* (1957). Uncertain about her identity as a Roman Catholic,

7

a religion that has always claimed to have the "truth," and distrustful of the novel as a vehicle for telling it, Spark creates a novel in which the protagonist, a convert, writes a novel while hearing voices either repeating her thoughts or formulating thoughts she will have.[5] Spark's distrust of the novel as a form reveals itself in her involved treatment in this work of the writing of the novel and its relationship to the writer's life.

Are our lives being written by an outside force, one of which we are unaware, just as the lives of the people in a novel are directed by the novelist? Is this outside force on our side or against us? Are we able to change the plot, or are we—like the characters—at the mercy of the force outside us? These are some of the underlying questions dealt with in *The Comforters*. Spark attempts to show the reader that there is a difference between life and art and that the two must not be confused, even though the novelist can manipulate the characters in complete control over them and the outside force can manipulate our lives in like manner.[6]

The novel opens as Laurence, a sports commentator who is visiting Mrs. Jepp, his grandmother, overhears her calling outside to the baker to leave her a "large wholewheat" because her grandson "won't eat white bread, one of his fads."[7] She insists on this order, even though Laurence shouts to her that he adores white bread and has no fads. Thus the fact that the grandmother lives at times her own reality, regardless of the literal reality, appears immediately. This underscores a basic theme of contemporary literature, the difficulty in communicating people's experience, as each person lives his or her own reality.[8] And Laurence, very observant, notices details unseen by others. In his childhood he had "terrorized" the household with his sheer literal truths" (4). These "literal" truths were unflattering facts he revealed about members of the household.

Although Mrs. Jepp lives in her own reality, when she does tell the literal truth, no one believes her. She talks of having a "gang," but the idea is so ludicrous that her family disregards it. Yet she literally communicates with her "gang" by carrier pigeon, thoroughly enjoying the intrigue of an illegal, yet satisfying, avocation in which smuggled diamonds are hidden in loaves of bread. The diamonds are then fenced in London. To Laurence is given the task of finding out how his grandmother can live in a much more luxurious fashion than her income would seem to allow. Mrs. Jepp, a thoroughly delightful character, always tells the literal truth about her own activities, but, locked into their own view of reality, members of her family refuse to believe her. She apparently enjoys her illegal game of smuggling for its excitement rather than for its monetary rewards.

The novel also focuses on Laurence's love for Caroline, a recent convert to Roman Catholicism, who is writing a book on the theory of the novel. She begins to hear typing and voices that repeat her thoughts or state thoughts that will come to her. There are parallels between Spark's life and Caroline's: the writing of a book, the recent conversion, the need to recover from a nervous disorder, to say nothing of the questions concerning the nature of art and reality that plague both Spark and her created counterpart. At a rest home Caroline meets Georgina Hogg, a monstrous caricature of a Catholic.

The plot swings between these two main threads: the gradual discovery of the truth about Mrs. Jepp's activities, and Caroline's attempt to solve the mystery of the voices at the same time as she attempts to find her own identity. But the weaving in of many other characters makes the plot also a study in interactions. Helene, Laurence's mother, a do-gooder, has secured a position for Georgina at Caroline's rest home. It is from Georgina that Helene learns of her mother's peculiar behavior, as Mrs. Hogg has opened a letter Laurence has sent Caroline and revealed the information about Mrs. Jepp that the letter contains. The London fence for the diamond-smuggling operation is a friend of Caroline's called "the Baron." The actual smuggler, Mr. Hogarth (who is aided by his crippled son), has been married to Mrs. Hogg and bigamously to a friend of the baron. The dense complications of the plot are due to the soap-opera fashion in which the characters interconnect. (And the interconnections mentioned represent only a sampling.)

The novel ends with good resulting from evil. The one truly evil character, Mrs. Hogg, drowns at a picnic while Caroline is trying to save her. Caroline knew that "if she could not free herself from Mrs. Hogg, they would both go under" (225). Caroline has had to free herself from evil, symbolized by the vicious nature of Mrs. Hogg, a born Catholic.

Mrs. Hogg disappears one other time. While riding to the picnic with Helene and the baron, she vanishes from the back seat. The baron and Helene turn around to talk to her, and she is not there. Then she reappears. Literally, she disappears by drowning; symbolically she disappears because she represents evil, which in the metaphysical order does not exist.

Further, Laurence comes to accept Caroline's symbolic truth and to reject his literal truth when he realizes that the letter he had written to Caroline and torn up before he sent it, has "got into the book" (233). Mrs. Jepp gives up smuggling and marries the baker, Mr. Webster, her former partner in crime. Young Hogarth's crippled legs are healed, and there is a suggestion that his part in providing cover for the smuggling (who would guess that a cripple being taken by his father abroad for a cure would be involved in smuggling?) enhanced his sense of self and resulted in his cure. Caroline and Laurence are to live happily ever after.

Because of the complicated nature of the question concerning truth as well as Spark's uncertainty about the relationship of truth to the novel, the themes in *The Comforters* are not readily apparent. The voices Caroline hears, the "comforters" of the novel's title are, in the beginning at least, as little comfort to her as Job's comforters are to him. Spark's wariness about the novel as an art form appears in her involved treatment of the voices, which are both within and without Caroline's control. Caroline refuses to believe that she is mad, despite the fact that she is the only one to hear the voices and that they cannot be recorded. The reader accepts that Caroline is not mad and accepts the existence of the voices, even though they are beyond normal experience. The supernatural, always an element in the Catholic religion, must be accepted, according to Spark, for faith means acceptance without proof, and Caroline is a believer.

Who or what the voices represent has been the subject of much scholarly conjecture. Peter Kemp believes that this is unfortunate "since the device here used, though locally amusing and ingenious, is finally not of much more than marginal importance."[9] But because the voices connect with both Spark's aesthetic and religious themes, they cannot be thus lightly dismissed.

At one point the voices tell Caroline that she and Laurence went by car to visit Mrs. Jepp before they have left for the trip. Caroline says to Laurence, "The narrative says we went by car; all right, we must go by train. You see that, don't you, Laurence? It's a matter of asserting free will" (108). But on reflection that it is a Holy Day of Obligation, requiring that she attend Mass, "her great desire to travel by train was dispersed by the obvious necessities of going to Mass. . . . 'The Mass is a proper obligation. But to acquiesce in the requirements of someone's novel would have been ignoble' " (110–11). Therefore, there appears to be a destiny guiding Caroline. Free will must be left untested because of the "proper obligation" of going to mass. And destiny has a serious accident in store for Caroline and Laurence, one in which Caroline is seriously injured. One must consider, therefore, the symbolism of the voices.

The voices appear to represent a being outside the normal being of each individual, who is in fact God, omniscient, but not necessarily controlling. The voices say that they will go by car, and they do. Caroline is not successful in attempting to rebel against the knowledge expressed by the voices, as she does what they predict she will do, after all. On the way to the car, Caroline tells Laurence that he is getting ideas through the "influence of a novelist contriving some phoney plot," that an attempt is being made to "organize" their lives "into a convenient slick plot" (115). She adds, "I refuse to have my thoughts and actions controlled by some unknown, possibly sinister being. I intend to subject him to reason. . . . I intend to stand aside and see if the novel has any real form apart from this artificial plot. I happen to be a Christian" (117). And then the crash comes, entangling Caroline in the wreckage.

But Caroline has done what she must after knowing all the circumstances. She was not free to choose before, as she was unaware of her mass obligation. It is more important (indeed, it is imperative) for her to follow the dictates of her religion (God's will), than it is for her to attempt to prove her free will. As a committed Catholic, she must follow the dictates of her conscience.

Caroline is the convert that Spark has become. She is convinced of her sanity despite the pressure her friends bring to make her feel that she is hallucinating. It is interesting to note, however, that the priest friend she visits treats her as normal, as "he seemed to assume simply that she was as she was" (65). Inflexible in her adherence to the tenets of Catholicism, she has little charity for the sinner, criticizing other people at times with great cynicism. Yet, in her refusal to believe that she is mad in hearing the voices, she exhibits complete acceptance of herself, independent of the opinion of others. Apparently she represents the model convert to Spark, one who is unwavering in her acceptance of the supernatural world of the spirits as well as determined to adhere to the truth of her religion.

If Caroline is the model convert, Georgina Hogg represents the evil born Catholic. Laurence points out in a letter to Caroline that they all "loathe" her, that she "suffers from chronic righteousness, exerts a sort of moral blackmail" (22–23). When Caroline first meets her at the rest home, she has "a pinching irritated sense of being with something abominable, not to be tolerated," and she has "a sudden intense desire to clean her teeth" (31). She thinks that Georgina "desires the ecstasy of murdering" her "in some prolonged, ritualistic orgy" because she sees that she is "angular, sharp, inquiring . . . grisly about the truth . . . well-dressed and good-looking" (32–33). Because of her loathing of Mrs. Hogg, Caroline feels that the "demands of the Christian religion are exorbitant, they are outrageous. Christians who don't realize that from the start are not faithful. They are dishonest. . . . These bemused patterers on the theme of love, had they faced Mrs. Hogg in person?" (38).

Unlike Laurence's mother, Helene, who befriends Mrs. Hogg and who, although not a Catholic, has a tolerance for her, Caroline sees only the hypocrisy in Georgina's Catholicism and is physically as well as intellectually repelled. The fact that she does her best to save Mrs. Hogg from drowning, and almost loses her life by so doing, represents her commitment in love to another, even though that other is completely repulsive to her. "She knew she would have to give Mrs. Hogg a hand into the boat. The anticipation of this physical contact, her hand in Mrs. Hogg's only for a moment, horrified Caroline. It was a very small thing, but it was what she constitutionally dreaded" (224). When Georgina loses her footing in getting into the boat and pulls Caroline into the water with her, Caroline does her best to save her, even though Mrs. Hogg is pulling her under. It is only because Caroline is able to hold her breath until the death grip on her neck loosens (because Mrs. Hogg has died) that Caroline lives. But the attempt to save Georgina's life reveals Caroline's intellectual commitment to her duty as a Catholic, despite her emotional loathing of the object her duty necessitates saving. Thus Caroline stands as a flawed, but committed, Roman Catholic.

Because Caroline is both a character in the novel and one who is spoken about by the writer of the novel, the point of view causes confusion. For example, "When her leg was not too distracting, Caroline among the sleepers turned her mind to the art of the novel, wondering and cogitating those long hours, and exerting an undue, unreckoned, influence on the narrative form from which she is supposed to be absent for a time" (155). It seems, therefore, that the actor is acting and being acted upon at the same time. When Caroline attempts to convince herself that the voices she hears are real, she tells her friend the baron, "The evidence will be in the book itself. . . . This physical pain convinces me that I'm not wholly a fictional character. I have independent life" (181–82). And finally, "her sense of being written into the novel was painful. Of her constant influence on its course she remained unaware and now she was impatient for the story to come to an end, knowing that the narrative could never become coherent to her until she was at last outside it, and at the same time consummately inside it" (206).

This confusion of point of view has the effect of distancing Caroline from the reader. Actions rather than motivations take center stage, so that there is no real insight into the characters. Caroline gives her opinion dogmatically, rather than revealing how or why she arrived at it. Spark's wit and repartee make the reading enjoyable, but the reader does not have much empathy with the characters. Mrs. Jepp, a lively old reprobate, amuses with her out-of-character actions and her daring to enjoy the dangerous. Caroline and Laurence, although likable for the most part, are not memorable. As in a soap opera, the presentation of the action pleases, but the viewer fails to gain any insight that would make the viewing stick.

Memento Mori

Continuing Spark's emphasis on the religious aspect of life, her next important novel, *Memento Mori* (1959), focuses on the primary goal of the committed Christian, death.[10] This novel of old age is dedicated to Teresa Walshe, a friend of Spark's and a nursing sister from whom she obtained details on the care of geriatric patients.[11] The author herself reveals her intention:

I decided to write a book about old people. It happened that a number of old people I had known as a child in Edinburgh were dying from one cause or another, and on my visits to Edinburgh I sometimes accompanied my mother to see them in hospital. When I saw them I was impressed by the power and persistence of the human spirit. They were paralyzed or crippled in body, yet were still exerting characteristic influences on those around them and in the world outside. I saw a tragic side to this situation and a comic side as well. I called this novel *Memento Mori*.[12]

The "power and persistence" of the human spirit informs this novel and makes it comic and tragic: comic in the humorous acceptance of the indignities of old age by the old people, and tragic in the sad necessity of those indignities. The reader responds with admiration rather than with pity, and as this is the exact reaction one human being desires of another, whatever the age, the fact that Spark achieves this in the reader attests to both her insight and her talent.

The three epigraphs of the novel emphasize the tragic-comic nature of the story:

> What shall I do with this absurdity—
> O heart, O troubled heart—this caricature,
> Decrepit age that has been tied to me
> As to a dog's tail?
>
> —W. B. Yeats, *The Tower*

> O what venerable and reverent creatures did the aged seem! Immortal Cherubims!
>
> —Thomas Traherne, *Centuries of Meditation*

> Q. *What are the four last things to be ever remembered?.*
> A. *The four last things to be ever remembered are Death, Judgment, Hell and Heaven.*
>
> —*The Penny Catechism*[13]

The tragic quotation from Yeats underscores the very real suffering experienced by the characters in *Memento Mori*, not only the inmates of the old folks' home but also those still managing to live outside. The second quotation becomes comic in the light of the "creatures" who people the novel. Far from "reverent," the old ladies of the home exhibit an earthiness and a humanity filled with the wit of their acceptance of, as well as their struggle against, the indignities forced upon them by their decaying bodies. The last quotation indicates the deep and serious subject of the novel. There is no more religious topic than the contemplation of death. The two ways of viewing death, the Christian and the pagan, show forth in this novel, which, although about death, emphasizes the indomitable human spirit.

The work opens with Dame Lettie Colston receiving, for the ninth time, an anonymous telephone call with the same message, *"Remember you must die."* Immediately after, Lettie's brother Godfrey Colston takes her to the home he shares with his wife, Charmian, who had been a popular novelist many years before. While at his home, he receives a telephone call which says, "Tell Dame Lettie . . . to remember she must die" (14). As no one outside knows that his sister is at his home, the calls must be seen on other than a natural level.

Other old people who still live outside nursing homes receive the same message, until the novel ends with a list of the deaths of the principal characters. The plot is slight, but complicated, shifting between the inmates of the home (who are called "grannies") and their struggle for dignified survival, and the outside friends of principally Miss Taylor, former companion to Charmian. For example, Charmian's husband, Godfrey, is being blackmailed by his housekeeper Mrs. Pettigrew. It is only when Miss Taylor, from the nursing home, insists that Alex Warner (her one-time lover) tell Godfrey that Charmian has also been guilty of infidelity and cites actual places and dates, that Godfrey is free from the blackmail.

Because of the complexities of the plot and the characters' interactions with one another, a short description of the principal characters and explanation of their part in the plot, if important, follows. Henry Mortimer, a retired policeman and Jean Taylor will be discussed last, as they represent Spark's own view. They both represent mature, good people, even though in Spark's opinion, Jean Taylor, as a Catholic convert, might be expected to, and Henry Mortimer, as an unbeliever, might not.[14]

Guy Leet, lover of Charmian and still apparently maintaining his sexual charm despite having to walk with two canes, is writing his memoirs. His snide references to the poet Ernest Dowson so enrage his aged friend Percy Mannering, also a poet, that he actually comes to blows with him. But after the altercation, Guy not only accepts his friend's dinner invitation, but he stays with him at his home for three weeks. This type of scene, played many times in the novel, gives the story a playful, as well as witty, cheerful, air.

Percy Mannering, a vivid, robust poet, uses even the fearful anonymous telephone messages as subject matter for a poem. The affectionate portrayal of this old poet reflects Spark's affection for the late Herbert Palmer, a poet friend who served as model.

Godfrey Colston, an unpleasant character, jealous of his wife Charmian, has bullied her because of her success as a novelist. "It was not that he wished his wife any harm, but his spirits always seemed to wither in proportion as hers bloomed. . . . Everyone making a fuss over Charmian, as if she were still somebody and not a helpless old invalid— roused within him all those resentments of the long past; so that, having made the mistake of regarding Charmian's every success as his failure, now, by force of habit, he could never feel really well unless she were ill." (158–59). Olive, friend of Godfrey's son Eric, and Percy Mannering's granddaughter, supplies the erotic satisfaction required by the salacious Godfrey. She displays for him, for a fee, the part of her thigh at which garter and stocking meet. Eventually, Mrs. Pettigrew, his scheming, blackmailing housekeeper takes over the task.

Godfrey, pictured as the typical bully, jealous, resentful, insecure, pursues his shoddy erotic occasions and, for his own selfish ends, attempts to keep Charmian from going to live in a nursing home where she will be happier and free from the suspicion that Mrs. Pettigrew is trying to poison her. He allows Mrs. Pettigrew to blackmail him, not because the revelation of his past indiscretions might hurt Charmian, but rather in order not to allow Charmian to have moral superiority over him. Of course, when he learns that she has been just as "immoral" as he in the past, he is delighted and feels "unaccountably healthier than he had been for some months" (184). He seems to be afraid of "some superiority in Charmian and the loss of his pride before her" (16). In his egocentricity and in his jealousy of his wife, he appears as a completely dislikable person. Furthermore, Charmian thoroughly dislikes him.

Unlike her husband, Charmian Colston is charming, sane, and witty. Once a popular novelist, she now finds that her mind fails her at times. Yet she pretends to be the victim of this failure more often than she really is. She realizes the threat that Mrs. Pettigrew poses to Godfrey, and she thinks about going to Godfrey and telling him that there is nothing about his past life that would surprise her, but "she did not possess the courage to do this. He might . . . turn on her. . . . What new tyranny might he not exert to punish her knowledge?" (162). She muses about her relationship with Godfrey, "over the humiliations she had received. . . . Never had she won a little praise of recognition but she had paid for it by some bitter, petty, disruptive action of Godfrey's" (162–63). But she does not have the courage to leave him. She stays with him instead of going into the nursing home as she longs to do.

The reader might wonder why the charming, perceptive wife submits to the tyranny of a jealous husband to the extent that she will not even leave him for a nursing home, but Charmian is a Roman Catholic. Although Spark does not emphasize the relationship between husband and wife as a sacred one (and certainly Charmian would not be committing a sin in the eyes of her church if she left Godfrey for the peace of a nursing home), yet the obligation as represented by the marriage vow apparently looms large in her life. It is only when she believes that Mrs. Pettigrew would go so far as to poison her (a justified suspicion, given the character of Mrs. Pettigrew) that she determines to go into the home, a place in which she is deeply content.

Alec Warner, former sociologist, visits Miss Taylor in the nursing home often. He spends his time keeping an elaborate card file on his old acquaintances, complete with cross-indexing. He records their reactions to stress as well as any other facts he can prevail upon them to give him. He is careful to ask Godfrey to record his reactions while reading the letter about Charmian's past infidelities, which he had sent him at Miss Taylor's instigation. His preoccupations with such reactions in the midst of small crises afford a humorous, if satiric, look at the minds of sociologists. Aside from his fixation on his card file, Alec Warner appears as a mature, even a good, person. But his records are his life. When they are destroyed in a fire, he feels that he is "already dead, since his records had ceased to exist" (222).

Peripheral to these characters, all of whom live outside the home, is Dame Lettie Colston, Godfrey's sister, the first and principal recipient of the voice warning, "Remember you must die." Presented as a selfish, suspicious character, she even includes a friend, former Chief of Police Henry Mortimer, in her list of those who may be The Voice. She, along with the others, has enlisted his aid in solving the mystery.

But the frightening pronouncement that she has heard so often becomes the means of her death. Because of her fear of hearing The Voice, she has her telephone disconnected. She also makes a paranoid search of her house every night before retiring. Her maid Gwen, amused by these actions and by Dame Lettie's refusal to inform the police, actions the maid attributes to a deranged mind, tells her boyfriend about them. He repeats what he considers a good story to some of his friends. The conversation is overheard by a laborer who recounts it to a window cleaner who pays for such leads. Thus, Dame Lettie's house becomes marked for robbery. Waking up in .the midst of the break-in, she is bludgeoned to death by one of the thieves. Ironically, her morbid fear of death has led directly to her death, a horrible one. And the involved means by which the burglar learns of her vulnerability indicates the mischievous wit with which Spark characterizes Dame Lettie, who trusted the wrong people and feared the wrong things. "Where violent death might, in tragedy, result from a character's attempt to rise above the common, in satire it is the product of pettiness, evil and accident."[15] Godfrey Colston's death *(The Comforters)* and Sir Quentin's death *(Loitering with Intent)* are satiric in this sense also. Lise's death *(The Driver's Seat)* is the epitome of satire.

Unlike Dame Lettie, Henry Mortimer and Jean Taylor do not fear the dire warning of The Voice, and their deaths are relatively peaceful. They both stand as realists. Henry tells the group assembled to enlist his aid that if he had his life to live over again, he would "form the habit of nightly composing" himself to thoughts of death. He tells them that there is "no other practise which so intensifies life. Death, when it approaches, ought not to take one by surprise. It should be part of the full expectancy of life. Without an ever-present sense of death life is insipid. You might as well live on the whites of eggs" (153). When questioned as to what he believes is the motive and who the author of The Voice, Mortimer replies that the motive may be different in each case and that "the offender is . . . whoever we think he is ourselves" (155). As Mortimer apparently speaks for Spark, on the deepest level the novel implies that life must be lived for death; for death, in the religious view that Spark espouses, is not the end but rather the beginning of life.

Like Henry Mortimer, Jean Taylor represents Spark's opinions. She is, by far, the most sane and the most Christian of the characters. Eighty-two years old, she had been a companion-maid to Charmian until her arthritis was so bad she could no longer walk comfortably. Upon admittance to the home the previous year, she had felt miserable being addressed as "Granny," objecting, as many of the old people did, to this disrespectful form of address. But because she was "a woman practiced in restraint," she never showed how she felt. Yet when the nurse treats her like a child one night, she feels "the pain of desolate humiliation so that she wished rather to endure the physical nagging again." After a year in the home, she resolves to "make her suffering a voluntary affair. If this is God's will then it is mine." She gains a "visible dignity" from this, but she loses her "stoical resistance to pain" (17), complaining more frequently and even, on one occasion, wetting the bed when the nurse takes a long time to come. The paradox inherent in her state of mind—on the one hand doing God's will by accepting her suffering, and on the other, losing her resistance to pain— indicates that the acceptance of God's will does not necessarily carry with it all benefits.

Miss Taylor spends much time "considering her position." When the doctor greets her with "Well, how's Granny Taylor this morning? Have *you* been making your last will and test—," he falters when he sees her eyes, noting "the intelligence." She hates these visits and the nurse telling her she "looked like sixteen," but "she volunteered mentally for them, as it were, regarding them as the Will of God. She reflected that everything could be worse . . . and the time would surely come for everyone to be a government granny or grandpa, unless they were mercifully laid to rest in their prime" (17–18).

Jean Taylor is the pivot around which the characterization of the grannies in the ward turns, as well as the central representation of Spark's religious views. Like Spark, she is a convert, having followed her employer, Charmian, into Roman Catholicism. Apparently her conversion has become central to her life, as it has for Spark. Further, Jean Taylor, like Henry Mortimer, has her own idea of the author of *The Voice*. During one of Dame Lettie's visits, Jean tells her, "the author of the anonymous telephone calls is Death himself. . . . I don't see . . . what you can do about it. If you don't remember Death, Death reminds you to do so. And if you can't cope with the facts the next best thing is to go away for a holiday" (179). Of course Lettie does not take this good and sane advice. If she had, she would not have been home at the time of the burglary, thus avoiding a violent death.

Jean Taylor's point of view obtains, except when the point of view is objective. Spark's tone is tender in presenting the old people in their comic-tragic situation. Although none of them has the astuteness and the honesty of Jean Taylor, all struggle to maintain their egos in attempting to survive the indignities forced upon them by the aging process as well as by the lack of understanding of those in charge.

One of the outstanding fearless grannies is Miss Jean Barnacle who "had no birth certificate but was put down as eighty-one, and who for forty-eight years had been a newsvendor at Holborn Circus" (15). This is an example of Spark's ironic use of material. The contrast between the lack of a birth certificate for one whose job it was to dispense facts as well as the contrast between the aged (useless) person and the occupation she had held (important job—dispenser of news) point up Spark's underlying cynicism and cause the reader to reflect on the ironic result of the aging process.

And Granny Barnacle brings lively humor, wit, and real help to the "Maud Long Medical Ward" of twelve females, called "Baker's Dozen" by the ward sister who does not know that "this is thirteen but having only heard the phrase; and thus it is that a good many old sayings lose their force" (15). It should be noted that these added meanings by the author abound, and although the words are light and not dwelled upon, the added dimension colors the entire sentence. Through Granny Barnacle's persistence and courage, Sister Burstead (called Sister Bastard for obvious reasons) is finally removed from the ward. When the new sister catches Granny Green "absentmindedly scooping the scrambled egg off her plate into her locker," and says, "What the hell do you think you're doing," Granny Barnacle remarks, "That's how I like them" (112–13). What she likes is treatment that respects the individual, and to be called to task for doing a silly thing comes under that category.

Granny Barnacle enlivens the ward with her wit. When Granny Valvona, who knows the birth signs of each of the grannies and reads their horoscope each day (and remembers and remarks when one of the predictions comes true), announces that her horoscope indicates that Granny Barnacle will show her originality, Granny Barnacle tells her, "Ho. . . . Originality today, I'll wear me britches back to front" (113). The inhabitants of the ward help the reader to see that human beings, their reactions and wit still intact, inhabit the outworn bodies.

The scenes in the ward do not lead to sentimentality or pity. Spark makes these old people individuals, and even when she shows the sad things they do, it is never depressing. There is an emphasis on the fact that despite the apparent indignities the body forces, the human spirit survives and wishes to be treated as maturely human, not as a child. One does not wish to be pitied or talked down to but rather respected and loved. When Granny Barnacle dies, Miss Valvona and Miss Taylor attend a mass for her with three other grannies from the ward who are not Catholics, but who had been "attached to Granny Barnacle in various ways, including those of love, scorn, resentment and pity" (120). Here Spark again catches the reader off guard, as the "various ways" of attachment ordinarily do not carry the connotation of "scorn" and "resentment." Granny Barnacle has carried her individuality to the grave, and she certainly is not considered one of the "Immortal Cherubims" of Thomas Traherne by those attached to her by "scorn" and "resentment."

Near the end of the novel, Granny Bean celebrates her 100th birthday and, satirically, Spark records the questions and answers asked from time immemorial on such an occasion, such as "What does it feel like to be a hundred?" and the weak answer "All right!" (220). Miss Valvona reads for the third time that day, "September 21st—today's birthday. Your year ahead: You can expect an eventful year. . . . It says here in black and white" (221). But Mrs. Bean is already asleep, with her mouth forming a small *0*. Again Spark accomplishes her purpose of satirizing both the interviews conducted on the aged and the believers in horoscopes. Mrs. Bean cares neither for airing her ideas on her long life nor knowing the prospects of her life in the future. Her mouth forming the small *0* as she sleeps attests to the carelessness with which she views both.

Unlike many who deal with the old, Spark never fails to accord these women the respect due them. She refers to them always as "Mrs." and "Miss." It is only when the point of view is that of the ward attendants that she uses the appellation "Granny." So she uses "Mrs. Bean," as does Miss Taylor when she tells Alec Warner about the birthday celebration.

Jean Taylor encourages Alec to start on his research again, but he feels he is too old. His assessment is that it was "an accumulation of years of labour. It was invaluable" (221). Of course this is not Spark's view, since she uses his investigation to satirize sociological research data that she believes to be for the most part useless.

The novel concludes, appropriately enough for a novel whose subject is death, with the death or final years of the main characters. For example, "Charmian died one morning in the following spring, at the age of eighty-seven" (223). This is a brief notice, but Charmian had lived a middle-of-the-road life, doing well for herself but not much of a help to others, although a fairly good person.

"Godfrey died the same year as the result of a motor accident. . . . He was not killed outright, but died a few days later of pneumonia which had set in from the shock. It was the couple in the other car who were killed outright" (223). Godfrey, even through his death, has injured others. Selfish in life, he remained selfish in death.

"Percy Mannering is in an old men's home, where he is known as " 'The Professor' " (223). Here he is treated with respect and is visited by his granddaughter Olive who takes his letters and poems, which she types and dispatches under his direction. As a poet, his life remains fulfilling. Refusing to give up his gift, he is not called upon to surrender his spirit along with the body.

"Chief Inspector Mortimer died suddenly of heart-failure at the age of seventy-three, while boarding his yacht, *The Dragonfly*" (223). He is spared the indignities of old age. He lived with the realization that death gave meaning to life. Although pagan in his beliefs, he lived a good and useful life. His death, sudden and in the midst of pleasure, is entirely fitting.

"Alec Warner had a paralytic stroke following a cerebral hemorrhage." He lives in a nursing home and "frequently searched through his mind, as through a card index, for the case histories of his friends, both dead and dying" (223–24). He recites to himself the list of the illnesses they died of, a satiric comment on the lists in Proust's *Remembrance of Things Past*. As his life, at least the latter part of it, was taken up with a concentration on reactions of his friends to stress, so he suffers the stress of his paralysis and recites to himself lists of useless facts.

"Miss Valvona went to her rest. Many of the grannies followed her" (224). Brief and to the point, the messages state that these old people died, and there is nothing left by which to remember them.

"Jean Taylor lingered for a time, employing her pain to magnify the Lord, and meditating sometimes confidingly upon Death, the first of the Four Last Things to be ever remembered" (224). As a good Christian, Jean Taylor, the convert, is faithful to Christian tenets to the end. And the emphasis on her death fittingly in the last paragraph of the novel, underscores the novel's religious theme. Spark's vision can be best understood by examining the characterizations of Henry Mortimer and Jean Taylor.

Mortimer is a person who lives existentially, celebrating life and accepting the knowledge that he must die. Having recently had a heart attack, he must watch his activity. Because of this, he feels close to death. When he tells the group assembled at his home, "To remember one's death is, in short, a way of life," he is only stating what his way of life has necessarily become. He denies that this is "a specifically religious point of view" (153). For him, professing no religion, it is not, but for Spark, convinced of the world's formation by God, this acceptance of death as giving meaning to life certainly is.

It comes rather as a shock to the reader to learn that Mortimer, the staid, gentle, sane policeman, has also received the mysterious call, as he did not mention this to the group who came seeking his help. After they leave, he answers the telephone, puts down the receiver, and thinks, "How strange . . . that mine is always a woman, gentle-spoken and respectful" (156). As Mortimer has expressed the idea that the "offender" is whoever each one thinks he is, the fact that the voice is that of a gentle, respectful woman indicates his belief, or his wish, that death itself be soft, gentle, and respectful.

In contrast to Mortimer, Jean Taylor stands as the committed Christian. Offering her suffering to God and continuously contemplating her last end, she lives in the knowledge that she is allowing God's will to take control of her life. She remains calm when Dame Lettie discusses the frightening telephone calls she has been receiving and tells her, "Perhaps you might obey it" (39). It is what she herself does—obeys the stricture to remember her death. It is the basis of her life, not for the reason given by Mortimer, to make life meaningful, but for the reason of the Penny Catechism, because death is the culmination of life in the return of the individual soul to God.

When Alec Warner, true to his sociological disposition, finds out that Granny Green has died, he asks Miss Taylor, "Now what was Granny Green?" For him, the person is what she died of. He questions further, wanting to know "whether a death is a good or bad one" and asking her to "keep a look out." And for that moment, Miss Taylor "utterly hated him," but she replies that a good death "doesn't reside in the dignity of bearing but in the disposition of the soul." When he tells her to "prove it," she "wearily" replies, "Disprove it," and he changes the subject (170–71). This scene emphasizes the direction of Jean Taylor's life. Founded on the truths of the Catholic church, truths to which she has committed herself in becoming a Catholic, she remains interested in life as a preparation for reward or punishment after death. Her weariness indicates that one gets tired of being asked to prove the unprovable. Faith means acceptance without proof.

In addition, when Alec tries to get her to join Charmian in the nursing home, apparently one in which the inhabitants are not senile, she tells him that she cannot leave her old friends. When he says, nodding toward the senile group, "And this?" she replies, "That is our memento mori. Like your telephone calls" (172). Living with the old and feeble, Jean Taylor finds them capable of enhancing her chances for heaven. As a committed Catholic, she accepts God's will, offers her sufferings to God, and remembers that she will have to account for her life, which she has lived according to the belief that God rules the universe, that things happen according to His will. There is no quarrel, either for her or for Muriel Spark, with this view.

Memento Mori has been called a "small masterpiece," as Spark has, for the first time, "her theme, her characters, all the techniques of her craft under her control." It "presents the characters from the inside."[16]

It has also been called her "most lyrical and the most religiously assured" of her works.[17]

Nevertheless, the characterization remains on a superficial level, inasmuch as one gets an idea of the characters and forms an opinion without actually getting to know their motivations, hopes, dreams, or other aspects that would make them truly memorable. The reader can intellectually follow the ideas imaged in each character, but the emotional impact does not follow. Instead, one is brought up short by the unexpectedness of the idea, as illustrated in the way her friends are said to have remembered Granny Barnacle, with "scorn" and "resentment," as well as the more usual love and pity.

These unexpected about-faces lead the reader to detect in the novel a cynicism bordering on pessimism. And even though the characters are exhorted to remember that they must die, no one changes in any way. The three characters who are able to contemplate dying with equanimity (the two converts, Charmian and Miss Taylor, and the retired policeman, Henry Mortimer) see dying according to their own basic vision, a vision that does not change: the converts in the conventional religious way view it as the culmination of life, and the policeman as "part of the full expectancy of life" (153).

Critic Peter Kemp looks upon the telephone voice as "the witty updating of a literary convention, a convenient, if baroque, way of transmitting those intimations of mortality with which the novel is concerned, the mysterious caller only puts into plain words a message already sounding, at one level or another, in the minds of all his hearers."[18] But the voices appear to be more than a literary convention. They relate directly to the character of each hearer.

For Derek Stanford, this book marks the beginning of the author's trading of the humanity of her characters for "external hall-marks, tricks of speech, oddities of gesture, surface idiosyncrasies. 'I am eccentric: therefore I am' becomes the existential formula for her characters."[19] This cannot be denied; the use of idiosyncrasy often leads the reader to remember the eccentricity rather than the character. But in *Memento Mori*, the effect is cumulative, so that one remembers the positive aspects of old age rather than the depressing ones: the spunk of Granny Barnacle, the intelligence of Jean Taylor, the gentleness of Charmian, the vitality of Guy Leet and his lingering sexual attraction despite the two canes with which he propels himself.

Thus, although the entire subject of the novel is death and the cast of characters represents old age, the underlying cynicism of society's response to both is relieved by the characters themselves who refuse to pity themselves and refuse to allow anyone else to pity them. And the pessimism is redeemed by the "two attitudes the book endorses: the religious view, seeing death as an end in which there is a crucial beginning . . . and a more pagan interpretation, in which it is again redeemed from terrifying absurdity by seeming to belong to some necessary cycle."[20] But as pointed out, the more "pagan interpretation" does not exclude the religious view that God's grace may operate even in the nonbeliever.

The Bachelors

Turning from the contemplation of the aged, Spark devotes her next novel (1960) to a group of younger characters, London bachelors. Again her wit and satire work to present a cross section of society, stereotyped to a certain extent, but nonetheless drawn as a clear picture of what she considers good and evil. As in the novels previously discussed, the plot does not contain a single story line but rather intermingles the characters. Even those who are not acquainted at the beginning, through the force of events, do become involved with each other before the conclusion.

Calling London "the great city of bachelors," Spark opens with a vignette of the occupants of single apartments: "In Queens Gate, Kensington, in Harrington Road, the Boltons, Holland Park, and in King's Road, Chelsea, and its backwaters, the bachelors stirred between their sheets, reached for their wound watches, and with waking intelligence noted the time; then, remembering it was Saturday morning, turned over on their pillows. But soon, since it was Saturday, most would be out on the streets, shopping for their bacon and eggs, their week's supplies of breakfasts and occasional suppers; and these bachelors would set out early, before a quarter past ten, in order to avoid being jostled by the women, the legitimate shoppers."[21] At the very beginning, there is the hint that the bachelors are somewhat outside the norm, not the "legitimate" inhabitants of the stores. Certainly the most important bachelor is Ronald Bridges, age thirty-seven and assistant curator of a small museum of handwriting. Ronald, an epileptic, had wanted to be a priest, but his disability precluded it. Still he has taken on many of the attributes of the priesthood, particularly in helping his friends when they come to him for advice. "Ronald in all his actions is fruitful, giving, generous; he reserves his mockery of his friends for his own private thoughts, and even there he counters his 'demonology' by enumerating the good qualities as well."[22] And he maintains an aggressive independence in spite of, or perhaps because of, his disability. The plot develops around him.

Ronald becomes involved with members of a spiritualist society because the main spiritualist, Patrick Seton, is about to be tried for defrauding a widow, Freda Flower, of her life savings. Ronald is drawn in because the prosecuting barrister is his bachelor friend Martin Bowles (who himself is defrauding his friend Isobel) and because he is called to testify as a handwriting expert.

Patrick Seton is fiercely defended by Alice Dawes (pregnant with Patrick's child) and Marlene Cooper, leader of the spiritualist circle, "The Wider Infinity." Marlene alleges that Patrick has succeeded in contacting her dead husband. Patrick intends to kill Alice with an overdose of insulin, obtained through his blackmail of a doctor, Dr. Lyte. If he is acquitted of the charges of fraudulent conversion, Patrick plans to take Alice to the doctor's remote chalet in Austria and cause an apparent accident to Alice, because she has become a bother to him.

In addition to Patrick Seton, another spiritualist, Mike Garland, charlatan, pimp, procurer, and his buddy Father Socket, a pseudoclergyman, also engage in illegal and immoral activities. Elsie Forrest, Alice's friend and roommate, spiritually in love with Father Socket, finds out that Ronald Bridges has a forged letter that will help convict Patrick. She steals it from Ronald's flat and takes it to Father Socket. Arriving at his flat, she is confronted by Mike Garland in striped bathrobe and wearing lipstick. Concluding rightly that these men are homosexuals, she feels betrayed and gives the letter back to Ronald. Further, at the last minute, her testimony that she had been with Father Socket at the time he said he had been with Patrick Seton, results in the conviction of Patrick. The novel ends with the promise of a forthcoming investigation of the activities of Father Socket. There is also the promise of marriage between Alice Dawes and Matthew Finch, London correspondent of the *Irish Echo,* who has been in love both with Alice and with the fact that she is pregnant. As the novel ends, Ronald walks around his flat, discharging his demons, and the final paragraph returns to the image of the bachelors introduced at the beginning of the novel.

The slight plot does not convey the novel's wry cynicism and satiric look at spiritualism and its followers. This can be better seen by examining some of the more important characters.

Ronald Bridges, by far the most moral, a Christ-like character, apparently bespeaks Spark's own vision of a world fallen from grace. Fourteen years previously, he had gone to America to a specialist experimenting with a new drug. He learned that his epileptic seizures would be intermittent, that he could prepare for them, but that he could not control them. He realized then that he could never be what he calls "first-rate," but he says, "I'll be a first-rate epileptic and that will be my career" (15).

The new drug does not work successfully on him, and he comes to think of himself as "one possessed by a demon, judged by the probing inquisition of life, an unsatisfactory clinic-rat which failed to respond to the right drug." As time went on, his experience "sharpened his wits, and privately looking round at his world of acquaintances, he became, at certain tense moments, a truth machine, under which his friends took on the aspect of demon-hypocrites. But being a reasonable man, he allowed these moods to pass over him, and in reality he rather liked his friends, and gave them his best advice when, in the following years, they began to ask him for it" (16).

His acceptance of himself in full humility (the hallmark of a saint) and of his friends despite their "demon" quality, make him a Christ figure. Courageously, he trains himself to maintain some sort of consciousness while enduring his seizures, attempting to look objectively at them rather than to surrender fully to their power. After approximately five years, the seizures have diminished in frequency to about one a month. He takes care of himself during his seizures, lives alone, gains a reputation in detection of forgeries, and is often called upon to testify to the authenticity of a document. So he settles down "to be an amiable fellow with a gangling appearance, slightly hunched shoulders, slightly neglected-looking teeth and hair going prematurely grey" (19).

After having been told by the doctor that he could marry the "right" girl, he had met Hildegarde, whose "wonderful understanding of his fits terrified him as much as her beauty moved him." She was "brown, healthy, shining, still in her teens and splendidly built. For two years she washed his socks and darned them, counted his laundry, did his Saturday shopping, went abroad with him, slept with him, went to the theatre with him" (19). But he gave her up because she told him he was a "genius" when he remonstrated with her for having wanted to obtain theater tickets to save him trouble. He told her he could well obtain them because he was not an "imbecile."

For it was an indulgent and motherly tone of voice which told him he was
a genius, and he saw himself being cooked for, bought for, thought for,
provided for, and over-whelmed by her in the years to come. He saw, as
in a vision, himself coming round from his animal frenzy, his limbs still
jerking and the froth on his lips—and her shining brown eyes upon him,
her well-formed lips repeating as he woke, such loving patronising lies as:
"You'll be all right, darling. It's just that you're a genius." Which would
indicate, not her belief about his mental capacity but her secret belief in the
superiority of her own. (21)

Rather than become less than the mature adult he knows himself to
be, Ronald ended the affair, which could have resulted in marriage and
having a mother for life, and lives the independent, wholesome life of
a morally good person, observing, but not outwardly condemning, his
friends. He attempts always to do the right thing, but he does not
force his views on others.

The one character who grows in wisdom and morality, Elsie Forrest,
does so through his influence, although it is what he is, rather than
through any preaching or exhortations on his part, that influences her.
Elsie Forrest seeks a spiritual relationship with a man rather than a
sexual one, even though she realizes that she is a very sensual woman.
This seeking had led her to the unfortunate relationship with Father
Socket. She accepts an invitation from Ronald's friend Matthew Finch,
a scrupulous Catholic, to visit him in his flat. In a comic episode,
Matthew eats onions in an attempt to keep the young woman away
and thereby avoid temptation. But she tells him she does not mind
his onion breath and goes to bed with him, giving herself satisfaction
and giving him a guilty conscience. But despite her acceptance of his
onion breath Matthew does not feel attracted to her, and instead falls
in love with her friend Alice, whose pregnancy makes her charmingly
alluring to him.

When Ronald attempts to make Elsie give back the forged letter
she has stolen from him, the letter that will help convict Patrick Seton,
he tells her she should give it back for the simple reason that it is not
hers. He believes one should act in a certain way because it is right
to do so. Right, of course, for Ronald and for Spark, means following
the commandments of God and the precepts of the Catholic church,
something most Catholics do not do, in the eyes of both Spark and
her character Ronald. He says, "As a Catholic I loathe all other Catholics.

. . . To me being Catholic is part of my human existence. I don't feel one way as a human being and another *as a Catholic*" (82).

Ronald refuses to promise Elsie that he will come back and talk to her again if she gives him the letter. He merely states that he will try to get it back from her again, if she refuses to give it up now. When she accuses him of talking like a friend and trying to sway her to do as he wishes, he tells her that he is a stranger, not a friend. Knowing that if she gives him the letter, there will be no chance of her seeing him again, she still gives it up. His matter-of-fact manner and the knowledge that he cannot be blackmailed force the better part of her nature to come to the fore. She gives him the letter, telling him to take it and to go quickly before she changes her mind. But instead, he sits down and examines the letter, and they discuss the case. He has confidence in her ability to do the right thing, and she does it. His integrity has been catching.

The most evil of the characters in the novel is Patrick Seton. There is an indication that he is not quite normal in his perception of reality, which makes him head the list of Ronald's "demons," people who fail to do what is right. Although he has been told by psychologists that his childhood had been a bad one, Patrick feels rather that it had been the only good time of his life. He feels that something has been wrong ever since then, and "the dream of childhood still remains in his mind as that from which everything else deviates" (159).

Not recognizing human laws or dogmas, Patrick Seton goes through life dreaming, reciting poetry, living in a childhood world of no responsibility, while at the same time avoiding occurrences that will disturb his peace. When a former girlfriend was going to have his baby, he simply moved away. Now that Alice is similarly pregnant, he plans to murder her, telling himself that he is going to release her spirit, that she really wants to be murdered.

Further, he sees himself as entitled to whatever he can fraudulently gain through his spiritualistic endeavors, and his many prison sentences have not changed his perception. And he is clever. He is "unaware what precisely was the deep secret in Dr. Lyte's career, to which he had given unconscious utterance one night in the seance room, the only occasion on which Dr. Lyte had attended a spiritualist meeting. Patrick, on coming round from his trance, had perceived the shaken stranger and had moved with fluttering obliquity towards him as a moth to the lamp." When Patrick, following this lead, calls on the doctor the next day and the doctor asks him where he got the information he

had hinted at in his trance, Patrick says "with mendacious truth" that
he does not know what the doctor is talking about (63). This, then,
provides Patrick with the means of blackmailing the doctor into giving
him drugs both to enhance his trances and to alleviate the effects of
them. His final blackmailing attempt results in his getting the doctor
to agree to let him use his chalet, difficult to reach in a secluded part
of Austria. This will be the setting for his murder of Alice.

Yet there are indications that Patrick does have some occult powers.
For example, an experimental drug that Dr. Lyte provides for Patrick
"greatly improved both the spectacular quality of Patrick's trances and
his actual psychic powers" (64). And there are also indications that
Patrick is able to influence Dr. Lyte to evil actions because the doctor
is already evil. When tempted to refuse Patrick the use of his chalet
because he is suspicious of Patrick's intended use of it, the doctor thinks
of his possessions, his practice, his daughter at Cambridge, his professional
friends, his vacation homes. "There was nothing he could think of that
he wanted to lose, and he regretted the evening he ever set foot in
Marlene's Sanctuary of Light" (91). Further, when he becomes more
certain of what Patrick intends to do, he writes him a letter, warning
him of the danger to Alice in any increase of her daily intake of insulin.
But he tears it up because of fear that Patrick, knowing that he suspects,
might reveal the secret for which Patrick is blackmailing him.

Ironically, Patrick knows nothing of the shameful event in Dr. Lyte's
past. He had only said at the seance (and this is another indication
that he does possess psychic powers) that "Gloria wishes to say she is
exhausted. . . . Gloria is tired. She feels weak. She is exhausted." It
is Dr. Lyte who, knowing the event, believes that Patrick knows it
also. For Gloria had died as a result of the illegal operation he had
performed, the abortion of a fetus that Dr. Lyte was not even sure
was his. He had not been implicated in any way. Gloria had said,
"I'm tired. I'm exhausted" after the operation. He himself became a
Communist for a while after "by way of atonement" (99).

The fact that Patrick, in his trance, used Gloria's name and the
actual words she spoke hint that Patrick's spiritual powers have some
validity. But Dr. Lyte believes that Patrick is a common blackmailer
and not a medium between this world and the next. He finds this less
frightening than believing that Gloria is actually sending him messages
from the grave. He rationalizes that Gloria must have told someone
the circumstances regarding her trouble and that somehow or other this

information reached Patrick. The doctor succumbs, therefore, to Patrick's blackmail.

But the ability of Patrick, if he is considered to be a "demon," to awaken guilt, has a good and a bad effect. It does force Dr. Lyte to consider his past actions and to pay for them, even though Patrick is the recipient of the payment. Had there been no past to hide, the demon would have had no power. In the next book discussed, *The Ballad of Peckham Rye*, the role of the demon is more fully explained.

For Ronald, the world is inhabited by demons. After the sentencing of Patrick to five years in jail, Ronald goes home to bed, only to awaken at midnight. He goes out to "walk off his demons."

> Martin Bowles, Patrick Seton, Socket,
> And the others as well, rousing him up: fruitless souls, crumbling tinder, like his own self which did not bear thinking of. But it is all demonology, he thought, and he brought them all to witness, in his old style, one by one before the courts of his mind. . . . Matthew Finch . . . and all the rest of them. He sent these figures away like demons of the air until he could think of them again with indifference or amusement or wonder. . . .

> It is all demonology and to do with creatures of the air, and there are others besides ourselves, he thought, who lie in their beds like happy countries that have no history. Others ferment in prison; some rot, maimed; some lean over the banisters of presbyteries to see if anyone is going to answer the telephone. (218–19)

Although "demons" are mentioned (and one might take these symbolically rather than literally) and there is a hint that some are gifted with psychic powers, Spark appears to be surer of her form than in earlier novels, because her plotting leaves out explicitly supernatural elements. Although there is a suggestion that there may be another dimension that only spiritualists can reach, this is offset by the idea that trances may be drug-induced and that most spiritualists are frauds. The plot, typically, swings back and forth between characters. It is dialogue that advances plot rather than action. The conversations between characters inform the reader of what is happening.

George Greene feels that it is "the challenge rather than the consolations . . . of religious faith" that concern Spark, and "hers is a God who encourages spontaneity more than ceremonial dignity and whose most sovereign power seems to stem from an urge to keep human beings in a state of surprise."[23]

Certainly Ronald Bridge's faith is severely tested through his disability, as Jean Taylor's *(Memento Mori)* is tested through hers. When asked whether he ever feels immoral by Matthew (who constantly does), Ronald replies, "Not very often. . . . I've got my epilepsy as an alibi" (81). He often has the type of seizure in which his drugs are of no use "after he had made some effort of will towards graciousness, as if a devil in his body was taking revenge" (116). He tells Matthew that the "Christian economy seems . . . to be so ordered that original sin is necessary to salvation" (88). The "revenge" of the devil, exemplifying the war between good and evil, points out the necessity of understanding the purpose of original sin. He resolves to go to confession "to receive, in absolution, a friendly gesture of recognition from the maker of heaven and earth, vigilant manipulator of the falling sickness" (116).

It is at a point such as this that Spark emphasizes the vulnerability of God's creatures. God is "friendly" but is also a "vigilant manipulator." No one rails about the unfairness of Ronald's affliction. It is accepted in humility as God's will, and Ronald displays a strong commitment to life, even going so far as to make himself stay awake during his seizures, a decision more painful than allowing himself to lose consciousness.

Ronald Bridges and Patrick Seton represent the battle between the demons and the God-centered. The world of Ronald Bridges is God-created; the world of Patrick Seton is self-created. The world of Ronald is the ideal whose foundations are Roman Catholicism; the world of Patrick Seton is a fallen one, whose foundations are not God but self.

Thus, in *The Bachelors,* Spark has advanced her skill in the novel, apparently losing her suspicion of it as an art form. She has also furthered her definition of the true Catholic as one who, in all humility, accepts oneself and one's place in God's world, and through being, rather than doing, manages to win the battle between good and evil.

The Ballad of Peckham Rye

Continuing to write of good and evil and demons, Spark changes the emphasis from a delineation of the good Roman Catholic to an examination of the demon in *The Ballad of Peckham Rye* (1960). The novel begins when Mavis, Dixie's mother, slams the door in the face of Humphrey Place who a few weeks earlier had literally left Dixie at the altar but who has now come back. A woman remarks that it would not have happened if Dougal Douglas had not come to town. There is speculation as to what really happened, but all agree that Humphrey answered "no" on his wedding day and came back later. The "affair is a legend referred to from time to time in the pubs when the conversation takes a matrimonial turn. Some say the bridegroom came back repentant and married the girl in the end. Some say, no, he married another girl, while the bride married the best man. It is wondered."[24] Such speculation continues, despite the fact that at the end of the novel, the reader learns, "In fact they got married two months later, and . . . quite a lot of people came to the church to see if Humphrey would do it again" (159). This confusion of reality, people who speculate while the reader is told that in fact they really know, underscores the subject of the novel, which has to do with illusion and reality and the gaining of knowledge.

The events start with Douglas Dougal's coming to Peckham Rye. An "Arts man," he has joined the firm of Meadows, Meade & Grindley, manufacturers of nylon textiles. He is to work on his own and "bring vision into the lives of the workers" (11). He is told that absenteeism is a problem. But under the guise of doing research, he himself manages to do no work at all. He also gets another job doing just as little with the firm of Drover Willis's, textile manufacturers. His work becomes the making of mischief, as he tells the workers to take a day off instead of finding out the cause of their absenteeism. He has a peculiar fascination for Humphrey Place who becomes his friend and for many others: notably his landlady, Miss Frierne; Old Nelly Mahone "who has lapsed from her native religion on religious grounds" (14), and who spies for Dougal, giving him information interspersed with her religious exhortations; Mr. Drury, his boss; and Merle Coverdale, Mr. Drury's mistress.

In addition to his two jobs (he is Dougal Douglas at Meadows, Meade & Grindley and Douglas Dougal at Willis's), he ghostwrites the autobiography of a Miss Maria Cheeseman, who lives across the river. To her facts he adds others, stories from Peckham, to make the book more interesting.

Dixie's brother Leslie, age thirteen, and his gang of juvenile delinquents steal two of Dougal's notebooks containing notes for Miss Cheeseman's autobiography. They are convinced that he is a spy and that the books contain code words. To frighten them and to get the notebooks back, he implies that he is a police spy. When this information gets about, both Mr. Drury and Mr. Willis give him a raise, even though he has made no attempt at blackmail. Spark implies that everyone hides guilty secrets and that it needs only a hint that someone will disclose them in order to cause the guilty one to pay.

Mr. Drury becomes obsessed with Dougal and pursues him in loverlike fashion, even attempting to get him to a rendezvous. Believing that his mistress Merle Coverdale is in league with Dougal (she has been typing the autobiography for him) and really hating her (as shown by his pinching, biting, bruising her under the guise of lovemaking), he stabs her nine times in the neck with a corkscrew, killing her, then puts on his hat and goes home to his wife.

After many altercations between Dougal Douglas and Trevor Lomas, friend of Humphrey Place, a young man who dislikes Dougal intensely, the story ends where it began, with Dougal Douglas leaving town and the townspeople making the events into a legend. Then the authorial voice comes in, and Humphrey drives off with Dixie. Dixie says, " 'I feel as if I've been twenty years married instead of two hours.' He thought this a pity for a girl of eighteen. But it was a sunny day for November, and, as he drove swiftly past the Rye, he saw the children playing there and the women coming home from work with their shopping-bags, the Rye for an instant looking like a cloud of green and gold, the people seeming to ride upon it, as you might say there was another world than this" (159–60).

Thus Humphrey implies that there is another world, the world of Dougal Douglas, a world in which people are urged to do what they wish to do, but when they do, harm befalls them. It suggests that freedom comes only from submission to God's will; apparent freedom comes from failure to submit and brings harm. Demons such as Dougal roam the world tempting humans to rebel. Dougal suggests freedom to others through his trite moralizing. Pictured as the embodiment of Satan, he brings woe to the world through a dangerous freedom.

Dixie, who blames Humphrey's initial defection at the altar on Dougal, exemplifies the typical eighteen-year-old small-town girl who, knowing that she is low on the class-structure scale, tries to rise in status through miserliness and hard work in order to amass enough money for a fine house. Humphrey, her lover, represents the average good young man intrigued by the charm and freedom of Dougal, who brings excitement to his dull life. But, after his act of rebellion in leaving Dixie at the altar, he returns to marry her and resume his ordinary life. His final thought indicates, however, that he now realizes that there are two worlds, the conventional one he has chosen and Dougal's world of excitement and danger.

Dougal's bosses, Mr. Drury and Mr. Willis, are typically ethic-stretching businessmen influenced by a popular idea that art and business should intermingle, that raising the sights of their employees will make them better workers. This is the idea that the humanizing power of art, brought to the business community, would result in workers more profitable to the business, apparently because they would see themselves as more than just cogs in a wheel. They are afraid of being found out in their own peccadilloes and are therefore ripe for the insinuations of Dougal. Like Patrick Seton, the fraudulent spiritualist who merely had to imply that he knew something of Dr. Lyte's past *(The Bachelors)*, Dougal has only to state trite moral truths, and the bosses, in their guilt, apply these to their own indiscretions. In this way Dougal can secure raises he does not deserve. In fact, the only result of his sojourn in Peckham Rye is the uprooting of ordinary values, the murder of Merle Coverdale, and the robbery of a till by Leslie.

Dougal, at the time of the actual wedding, never "read of it in the newspapers. He was away off to Africa with the intention of selling tape-recorders to all the witch doctors. 'No medicine man,' Dougal said, 'these days can afford to be without a portable tape-recorder. Without the aid of this modern device, which may be easily concealed in the undergrowth of the jungle, the old tribal authority will rapidly become undermined by the mounting influence of modern scepticism' " (158). His penchant for overturning basic values goes on, even in the jungles of Africa.

On his return from Africa, Dougal becomes a novice in a Franciscan monastery. "Before he was asked to leave, the Prior had endured a nervous breakdown and several of the monks had broken their vows of obedience in actuality, and their other vows by desire; Dougal pleaded his powers as an exorcist in vain. Thereafter, for economy's sake, he gathered together the scrap ends of his profligate experience—for he was a frugal man at heart—and turned them into a lot of cock-eyed books, and went far in the world. He never married" (158–60).

Dougal, the Satan character, becomes the author who achieves success through "cock-eyed" books. Spark's few comments on writers of fiction in this novel are telling. The autobiography of Miss Cheeseman, written by Dougal, contains fiction (lies). A devil who writes "cock-eyed" books is a successful author. Fiction fares badly.

Dougal's Satan character is revealed in the lumps on his head, which he asks people to feel, telling them they are the remains of horns that had been removed. In addition, one of his shoulders is higher than the other, giving him a hump-backed appearance. He tells Humphrey that he is "supposed to be one of those wicked spirits that wander through the world for the ruin of souls" (87). Mr. Weedin, under whom Dougal is supposed to work, tells Merle Coverdale, "It may surprise you. . . . But it's my belief that Dougal Douglas is a diabolical agent, if not in fact the Devil" (92). When walking through the cemetery with Merle, he "posed like an angel on a grave which had only an insignificant headstone. He posed like an angel-devil, with his hump shoulder and gleaming smile, and his fingers of each hand widespread against the sky." Merle looks "startled" (34). Again, when talking to Humphrey, he looks at him "like a succubus whose mouth is its eyes" (31).

Further, he has the ability to change into different roles as he acts out the situation confronting him. When Mr. Druce interviewed him, he "leaned forward and became a television interviewer," causing Mr. Druce to look at him "in wonder" (17). At Findlater's Ballroom, after dancing the Highland Fling and a Zulu dance, he "sat on his haunches and banged a message out on a tom-tom. He sprang up and with the lid on his head was a Chinese coolie eating melancholy rice. He was an ardent cyclist, crouched over handlebars and pedalling uphill with the lid between his knees. He was an old woman with an umbrella; he stood on the upturned edges of the lid and speared fish from his rocking canoe; he was the man at the wheel of a racing car" (67), and he continues his impersonations until stopped by the manager. And on a macabre level, when the brother that Miss Frierne does not wish to acknowledge is run over by a bus and killed, he says to her, " 'Ever seen a corpse?' He lolled his head back, closed his eyes and opened his mouth so that the bottom jaw was sunken rigid," making Miss Frierne scream "with hysterical mirth" (138). Satan, the master of deceit and disguise, becomes Everyman.

And finally, after Nelly begins to be suspicious of him and refuses the money he wants to give her for spying for him, he tells her he had a pair of horns like a goat when he was born. She says, "Holy Mary, let me out of here. I don't know whether I'm coming or going with you" (128). Later, when he comes out of a picture show, Nelly is outside declaiming words that fit Dougal exactly: "The words of the double-tongued are as if they were harmless, but they reach even to the inner part of the bowels" (148). And as he passes her, she spits on the sidewalk.

There can be no mistaking that Dougal represents Satan, the double-tongued Master of Mischief who stirs up a peaceful, if not a very moral, town. According to one critic, he "peddles a cure for life by encouraging people to turn their lives into fiction, into shoddy melodrama. He is a personification of evil not of death; the latter can be seen as a human good, and it is presented this way in *Memento Mori*."[25] Dixie, snobbish and penurious, cares only about enhancing her status; Merle Coverdale and Mr. Druce, in a pretense of love, blind themselves to their real feeling for each other until, culminating his hatred for her, he stabs her to death; Humphrey leaves Dixie at the altar; and the workers whose performance Dougal is supposed to help better, give in to their laziness. Dougal forces an awareness of reality by exposing each person's weak spot, ordinarily hidden under conventional behavior. But even if he succeeds in getting them to see more realistically, he offers nothing to curb the unleashed freedom: no self-control, no moral precepts.

Demons, therefore, roam the world. In this novel Satan himself takes human shape. Mischief becomes the paramount goal of his journey. According to Spark, each individual should face up to reality (knowledge) rather than succumb to his fictions. But the reality of knowledge is dearly bought. Spark retells the story of *Paradise Lost*.

The major theme of the novel, according to Peter Kemp, is "the way in which people are given to muffling truth with inauthentic words, editing reality for their own consolations." Dougal points out to Mr. Willis that his employees use the words "immoral" and "ignorant" very frequently. "What is significant about them," Kemp notes, "is that, camouflaging generalities, these vague, complacent adjectives—catchwords of a torpid tribe . . . are symptoms of real ignorance, true immorality."[26] This is certainly true. But added to this is the paradox implicit in the Fall, which involves a failure to assess reality properly, often through the use of language to cloud truth. This is underscored by Dougal's use of trite phrases and clichés in the autobiography he writes for Miss Cheeseman. The actress allows this distortion because she wants to avoid having unpleasant facts appear in the work. The clichés symbolize her fraudulent life because they literally camouflage truth. Dougal's intention, fundamentally, is to distort reality in order that the moral order be effectively masked.

Chapter Three
The Prime of
Miss Jean Brodie

In *The Prime of Miss Jean Brodie* (1961),[1] Spark's best-known novel, one that still is presented on the stage and in the cinema,[2] the author continues a characterization similar, in some ways, to that of Douglas Dougal in *The Ballad of Peckham Rye*. Jean Brodie, like Dougal, literally takes charge of the lives of others in a manipulation that is God-like (or Satan-like). Dougal's satanic traits do not appear outwardly in Miss Brodie, but her manipulation of others' lives is like his; both falsely assume God-like powers.

Added to the presentation of Jean Brodie as a prime manipulator is the depiction of the student-teacher relationship, which is presented as neither completely good nor completely bad, although it results in the betrayal of teacher by student. Finally, the weaving of plot and counterplot reveals *The Prime of Miss Jean Brodie* as one of Spark's most subtle and at the same time most understandable novels.

On the surface the plot appears to be a simple one. In 1930, the "Brodie Set," the six girls Miss Jean Brodie has chosen for her select few, are ten years old. She teaches them for only two years, but they remain hers, in one way or another, until they graduate from the Marcia Blaine School.[3] As in *The Ballad of Peckham Rye*, the plot weaves back and forth from the present into the future and back to the past.[4] Miss Brodie, always suspect by the school's headmistress for her unorthodox teaching, is forced to retire, betrayed by the one girl of the "Set" who she felt could not possibly betray her, Sandy. She dies of cancer at the age of fifty-six, after having revealed her love affair with the music teacher, Mr. Lowther, whom she had given up to enjoy vicariously a presumed love affair between Rose, one of her girls, and the art teacher, Mr. Lloyd, an affair she attempted to foster. Mr. Lloyd, she confesses, had been the love of her life. Sandy, her betrayer, becomes a Roman Catholic nun. It is she, not Rose, who has had an affair with Mr. Lloyd, who is a Roman Catholic and married. As a result, she lost interest in the man but became interested in his religion.

The story opens at the time the girls of the Brodie Set are sixteen. It moves back and forth between the time when they were ten until after Miss Brodie's death, when they are grown and talk to each other about her and about the time they were under her influence.

The girls do not fare as well as Miss Brodie had hoped. One, indeed, becomes a nun, which is as far away from what Miss Brodie would have hoped as possible. None are remarkable either in life or in accomplishments. Sandy has written a psychological treatise for which she has become rather famous, but when visitors come to see her at the convent, she grips the iron bars separating them. When she is questioned by someone about the greatest influence on her life during the thirties, she says, "there was a Miss Jean Brodie in her prime."[5] She "clutched the bars as if she wanted to escape"(52).

But in Miss Brodie's opinion, her girls are all famous for something. Monica Douglas is famous for mathematics and her hot temper. The reader last sees her when she comes to visit Sandy at the convent, having been sued for separation by her husband after throwing a live coal at his sister. Eunice Gardner is famous for her sprightly gymnastics and her swimming. She becomes a nurse, and twenty-eight years later, tells her doctor husband that she wants to visit Miss Brodie's grave, that Miss Brodie was a woman of culture and one of her favorites. She never learned that Sandy had betrayed Miss Brodie.

Rose Stanley is famous for sex, although this aspect of her personality is completely unknown to Rose or to anyone except Miss Brodie, until much later when Rose starts to attract boys and when Mr. Lloyd asks Rose to pose for him. Miss Brodie considers Rose to have instinct but no insight. But Miss Brodie's own insight appears faulty, as the affair she desires that Rose have with the art teacher takes place between him and Sandy instead. Rose later makes a good marriage and shakes off Miss Brodie's influence easily.

Mary Macgregor's fame "rested on her being a silent lump whom everybody could blame" (13). Mary became a shorthand typist and never thought much about Miss Brodie, never disliked her. She joined the Wrens in World War II where she was "clumsy and incompetent." Her first and last boyfriend, one she had known only two weeks, failed to show up for a date, and she never saw him again. At the age of twenty-four, Mary thinks back to the time when Miss Brodie's "stories and opinions which had nothing to do with the real world" was the happiest period of her life (24). She dies, while on leave, in a hotel fire, running back and forth between the flames at each end of the corridor, a death foreshadowed by her running back and forth in the science laboratory once while the class experimented with magnesium flares and flames shot out. At the time she ran back and forth between the benches until Miss Lockhart, the science teacher, told her not to be "so stupid" (113). Later, after Mary's death, Sandy wishes that she had been nicer to her. But, of course, she followed Miss Brodie's lead and treated Mary as the scapegoat also.

Jenny Gray, Sandy's best friend, wants to be an actress and later works toward this by attending a school of dramatic art. Her fame rests on her being the "prettiest" and "most graceful" of them (13). With Sandy, she writes a story of the supposed love affair between Miss Brodie and a young soldier, Hugh, presumably killed in World War I.

Sandy Stranger, the most important, is the one through whose eyes Miss Brodie is seen, when Spark, as the omniscient author, allows this. She is "notorious for her small, almost non-existent eyes, but famous for her vowel sounds" (12). Sandy's tiny eyes see more than the large ones of others. She sees through Miss Brodie and finally betrays her to the headmistress. The counterplot concerns her.

Although the story starts when the girls are sixteen and out of the form in which Miss Brodie taught them, and although they outwardly seem to conform to their new classes, they "remained unmistakably Brodie, and were all famous in the school, which is to say they were held in suspicion and not much liking." Their friendship with Miss Brodie remains the only thing that held them together, and Miss Brodie herself was "held in great suspicion" by the other teachers (11). Thus, at the very beginning of the novel, Spark creates an elite group under a leader distrusted by her peers. The girls themselves have nothing in common except their "friendship" with Miss Brodie. She has selected girls whose parents would not complain of the "more advanced and seditious aspects" of what she taught (39). They were taken to her home for tea, taken into her confidence, asked not to tell others the confidences she treats them to, told of her feud with the headmistress, and told that she endured her troubles for them, that now, in her prime, they were fortunate to be able to profit by her influence on them.

The impressionable ten-year-olds digest trite axioms masquerading as wisdom. Miss Brodie tells them that she is "putting old heads on your young shoulders" and that they are "the crème de la crème" (15). She tells them, "Speech is silver but silence is golden" (22), when she compliments them for not revealing to the headmistress that she has been telling them about her dead lover, Hugh, instead of teaching them history. Miss Brodie loves to proclaim trite quotations with an air of imparting great wisdom.

Her axiom "Give me a girl at an impressionable age and she is mine for life" (16) suggests the underlying themes of the novel, which concern what Miss Brodie teaches and its effect on the girls she has chosen to be hers. This can be seen by examining Miss Brodie through the eyes of Sandy who, along with Rose, is considered by Miss Brodie to be the best of the "crème de la crème."

As she tells the ten-year-olds about her last summer holiday, gives them hints on the care of the skin, relates an incident about a Frenchman she met in the train to Biarritz, describes Italian paintings she saw, Miss Brodie mixes her idea of culture with her own concerns. When she tells them that Giotto is the greatest Italian painter—"he is my favorite" (18)—she indicates the norm by which everything must be measured: herself. What she knows, what she does, what she thinks— all must be inculcated into the consciousness of these impressionable children. She convinces them that her prime has "truly begun." As one's prime is "elusive," one must recognize it at "whatever time of . . . life it may occur" and then "live it to the full" (18).

The dual nature of Miss Brodie can thus be seen in the first glimpse of her teaching. Her wish to broaden the vision of the youngsters is certainly a laudable one; but the determination to broaden it with her distorted version of reality suggests both her authoritarian nature and her desire to control. Her greatest wish is really to reproduce clones of herself.

Sandy, even at the age of ten, shows that she sees through the hypocrisy of Miss Brodie by making fun of the designation "crème de la crème" and by reflecting that these are supposed to be the happiest days of her life, even though Miss Brodie says that "prime is best" (25). Sandy, also, must lead a secret life in order not to be bored by Miss Brodie's recitations. She fantasizes, making up dialogue and scenes to entertain herself, indicating a tendency not to take Miss Brodie seriously. Sandy is admonished, during one of her fantasies in which she unconsciously screws up her face, to put on a composed look and think of the Mona Lisa who "in her prime smiled in steady composure even though she had just come from the dentist and her lower jaw was swollen" (33–34). Further, when Sandy, told to walk with her head "up, up," exaggerates by keeping her eyes on the ceiling, Miss

Brodie tells her that "one day" she "will go far" (35), which ironically foreshadows Sandy's betrayal of Miss Brodie.

Although Sandy sees more clearly into Miss Brodie's character than the others, she is also seduced by her. In a curious incident at the time of being told to walk with her head "up, up," Sandy mimics Miss Brodie and tells the scapegoat Mary Macgregor to walk with her head "up, up." Then she suddenly has a feeling of wanting to be kind to Mary instead of unkind in the way the rest of them are. But she hears Miss Brodie saying to Rose, "You are all heroines in the making," whereupon she looks at the group and sees them "as a body with Miss Brodie for the head" and as being part of Miss Brodie's destiny, "as if God had willed them to birth for that purpose." Then she becomes frightened at her desire to be "nice" to Mary Macgregor, because by this unorthodox action, she would "separate herself, and be lonely, and blameable in a more dreadful way" (45–46) than Mary who at least was part of the Brodie Set. Conformity is the price she must pay for being part of the set. So Sandy acts meanly towards Mary, then hates herself for it, then escapes into one of her fantasies, a married woman having an argument with her husband.

This shows the hold Miss Brodie has on even so perceptive a child as Sandy. Sandy has been made to feel special, a heady feeling, and she cannot give up Miss Brodie's control and thus be lost to the elite group formed by the teacher. There is nothing that can replace the excitement of being one of Miss Brodie's chosen. Conversely, nothing must come between her and the girls' loyalty to her. For example, Miss Brodie frowns upon the Brownies and the Girl Guides. Only she will form them; only she inspire them. In recalling Miss Brodie's admiration of Mussolini's marching troops, Sandy likens the Brodie Set to them, Miss Brodie's "fascisti," held together for her need. She feels that Miss Brodie does not want them to join the Girl Guides because she is jealous that the Guides would represent a "rival Fascisti." Then, when Sandy thinks that she might like to join the Brownies, "the group-fright seized her again," and she had to give up the idea, because she "loved Miss Brodie" (47–48).

The comparison of the girls to the fascisti becomes apparent to Sandy because Mussolini is one of Miss Brodie's heroes. She tells the girls that his fascists are "doing splendid things," and that he is "one of the greatest men in the world" (66). Miss Brodie's hero is, naturally, a fascist, as she herself is, recognizing as valid only what she so pronounces. Her confusion of values extends to open windows, which are "vulgar" if open more than six inches. Sleeves worn folded up because of the heat also represent vulgarity. Her personal likes and dislikes, her own decisions (even on minor matters) become of paramount importance to her, and by precept and example, to the girls in her charge. When she tells them about her visits to see the pope and A. A. Milne, the two are grouped together (along with Mussolini) by her description of her becoming clothes.

That Miss Brodie is attractive to others other than her girls becomes apparent to them when Monica sees Mr. Lloyd, the art teacher kissing her. Although Miss Brodie never becomes the lover of Teddy Lloyd, a married man, she does become the lover of Mr. Lowther, the music teacher. She uses Mr. Lowther, a bachelor, to get Teddy Lloyd out of her mind. Later when Sandy sits with Miss Brodie "shriveled and betrayed" (82), the whine in her voice—"betrayed me, betrayed me"—bored and afflicted Sandy. It is seven years, thought Sandy, since I betrayed this tiresome woman. What does she mean by "betray?" (89). Of course, Miss Brodie's meaning only pertains to herself. There is no thought of the betrayal of Mr. Lowther, who really loved her, or of Mr. Lloyd and his wife and family, or of the betrayal of the girls under her care. But as Sandy is not only bored but "afflicted" by the dying Miss Brodie, she has apparently never resolved her hate-love affair with her.

Miss Brodie attempts to play God in her desire to manipulate Rose and Teddy Lloyd into having an affair. She spends her weekends with Mr. Lowther, but she throws Rose and Teddy Lloyd together. When he helps Rose bring in some books, Miss Brodie thanks him for his help "as if she and Rose were one" (103). And indeed she is one with the girl in using Rose to satisfy Mr. Lloyd's love for her. All the portraits of Rose painted by Teddy Lloyd resemble Miss Brodie.

Sandy, while still under Miss Brodie's tutelage, has begun to see her underlying weakness. In describing Hugh, her dead lover, Miss Brodie tells them that he had artistic leanings, thus "making her new love story fit the old." Sandy is "fascinated by this method of making patterns with facts, and was divided between her admiration for the technique and the pressing need to prove Miss Brodie guilty of misconduct" (106). Sandy and Jenny had been writing fictional love notes between Miss Brodie and Gordon Lowther. As the end of the last term with Miss Brodie approaches, they bury this fictionalized correspondence in a cave, never again to see it. Sandy will no longer support the romanticized version of Miss Brodie.

But even when Miss Brodie loses them as students, they remain her set in the senior school. Knowing that she frowns on team spirit (because it dilutes their allegiance to her), they refuse to join teams. Also, she still entertains them at tea on Saturdays and asks that Sandy and Jenny teach her the Greek they are learning. Although the teachers in the senior school are indifferent to the girls of the Brodie Set, they recognize that the girls "display that capacity for enthusiasm" (123) that Miss Brodie had planted. Miss Brodie's influence has not been entirely negative.

And Miss Brodie extends her domination of the Brodie Set to Mr. Lowther, cooking and shopping for him to excess. Her visits to him are always on Sunday after church, any church at all except the Roman Catholic. She strongly disapproves of the Roman Catholic church because she feels that it builds on superstition and is embraced by people who do not "want to think for themselves." Spark points out that this is a peculiar attitude for Miss Brodie to have because she was "by temperament suited only to the Roman Catholic Church; possibly it could have embraced, even while it disciplined, her soaring and diving spirit, it might even have normalized her" (125).

This pointed analysis of Miss Brodie's temperament reveals some of Spark's own assessment of the religion she embraced. The disciplinary action of the Roman Catholic religion is self-evident, although there is a laxness in discipline (rules and regulations) stemming from the ascent to the papal throne of Pope John XXIII. Yet for the convert Spark, a strict interpretation of the commandments and the precepts of the church seems salutary. The church, for Spark, is the refiner of excess.

At any rate, Miss Brodie sees no incongruity in her pious Sunday worship in the morning and her love affair in the afternoon. She had no doubt that "God was on her side" whatever she did, being driven to "excessive action" by an "excessive lack of guilt." The girls of the Brodie Set were exhilarated by the feeling that they, in some way, "partook of the general absolution she had assumed to herself," and only in retrospect could they see Miss Brodie's love affair for what it was. While they were under her influence, Miss Brodie and what she did were "outside the context of right and wrong." And even after twenty-five years, Sandy recognizes that even though Miss Brodie lacked self-criticism, this "had not been without its beneficent effects" (126).

Even during vacation time the close connection between Miss Brodie and her girls cannot be forgotten, for the portraits Teddy Lloyd has painted of Rose, Monica, and Eunice, are all like Miss Brodie. When the artist wants to do all the Brodie Set together, Sandy thinks that this might be a means of denying the individuality of the members of the set, an individuality just beginning to emerge. She tells him that she supposes that they would "look like one big Miss Brodie" (150). After he kisses Sandy "long and wetly" and tells her that she is ugly, he says, "Jean Brodie . . . is a magnificent woman in her prime" (152). Miss Brodie has charmed not only the girls but also the art and music teachers, both of whom never fall out of love with her, even though Mr. Lowther, refused by Miss Brodie, marries the science teacher.

When Jenny does badly in her term examinations and all the portraits of the girls resemble Miss Brodie, Sandy has "the definite feeling that the Brodie set, not to mention Miss Brodie, was getting out of hand" (149). As Sandy begins to doubt Miss Brodie, ironically, she becomes the girl that Miss Brodie chooses to confide in. Miss Brodie's ambition is to have Rose become Teddy Lloyd's lover, while Sandy would keep her informed about the affair. Instead, Sandy becomes Lloyd's lover and Rose carries the information to Miss Brodie. Despite this, when Lloyd does paint the Brodie Set, each girl on the canvas represents a different Miss Brodie.

Sandy also begins to equate Miss Brodie with the Calvinism in her ancestry. She learns about Calvinism both through going about the previously forbidden part of Edinburgh alone and by reading John Calvin. In the city she begins "to look at the blackened monuments and hear the unbelievable curses of drunken men and women." She compares them with the "faces from Morningside and Merchisten" and sees "with stabs of new and exciting Calvinistic guilt" that they are similar (159–60). When she reads John Calvin, she finds that even though some people may misrepresent Calvinism, it was true that he had "made it God's pleasure" to make people erroneously joyful in their salvation, so that at the end their "surprise . . . might be nastier" (159). Even though Sandy could not "formulate these exciting propositions; nevertheless she experienced them in the air she breathed, she sensed them in the curiously defiant way in which the people she knew broke the Sabbath, and she smelt them in the excesses of Miss Brodie in her prime" (159). Miss Brodie, fundamentally Calvinistic in outlook, has made herself one of God's elect. Sandy begins "to sense what went to the makings of Miss Brodie who had elected herself to grace in so particular a way and with more exotic suicidal enchantment than if she had simply taken to drink like other spinsters who couldn't stand it any more" (160).

Sandy, analyzing Miss Brodie, finds that she "thinks she is Providence . . . she thinks she is the God of Calvin, she sees the beginning and the end. And . . . the woman is an unconscious Lesbian" (176). She also recognizes that all of Lloyd's portraits, even that of his smallest child, are turning out to be Miss Brodies. When she asks him why he has this obsession and why he cannot see that Miss Brodie is ridiculous, he replies that he does see that she is ridiculous. At this point Sandy's interest in Teddy Lloyd transfers itself to his mind; she is intrigued that he could be so obsessed with Miss Brodie, so much in love with her. So although she loses interest in him as a man, she becomes absorbed in trying to understand his mind, and "she extracted, among other things, his religion as a pith from a husk" (180). This leads to her embracing his religion and becoming a nun.

Sandy's desire to "put a stop to" Miss Brodie becomes foremost when Miss Mackay, the headmistress, tells her that Miss Brodie has formed a new set. Sandy advises Miss Mackay to examine Miss Brodie's politics, that she's a "born Fascist." Sandy confesses that she herself is not interested in politics, only "in putting a stop to Miss Brodie" (182). As a result of this conversation, Miss Brodie is forced to retire in 1931 for teaching fascism. Sandy remembers "the marching troops of black shirts" in the pictures Miss Brodie had put on her wall. But at that time she had already entered the Catholic Church, "in whose ranks she had found quite a number of Fascists much less agreeable than Miss Brodie" (183).

Miss Brodie never suspects that Sandy has given her away. She tells her that she is exempt from suspicion, as she had "no reason whatsoever" to betray her, and has had "the best part" of her "in her confidences and in the man" she loves. And Sandy replies, "like an enigmatic Pope: 'If you did not betray us it is impossible that you could have been betrayed by us. The word betrayed does not apply' " (185). Later, after Miss Brodie's death, Sandy tells Monica that one can only betray when one owes loyalty, and it was owed to Miss Brodie "only up to a point." She admits that Miss Brodie "was quite innocent in her way" and that she was "marvelous fun." And when a man comes to see her in the convent about the odd book of psychology she has written and asks her whether the main influences of her school days were literary, political, personal, or Calvinist, Sandy replies, "There was a Miss Jean Brodie in her prime" (186–87). This is the last line in the novel and as such adds to the enigma that is Miss Brodie and the enigma that is Sandy.

The interaction of Miss Brodie and Sandy forms the plot and counterplot. Jean Brodie, middle-aged spinster, fueled perhaps by the onrushing tide of authoritarianism reflected primarily in Mussolini, sees herself as weak, ineffectual, and unloved. She must convince herself that she can indeed be powerful, if only in her circle, the school in which she teaches. Spark places her in the category of "war-bereaved spinsterhood," those women who tried new ways of living, experimented with diets, joined popular causes, took courses, but "they were not school teachers" (64). Miss Jean Brodie, not unusual in her interests and pursuits, is unique in that she teaches them. And "there was nothing outwardly odd about Miss Brodie. Inwardly was a different matter" (64).

Inwardly, Miss Brodie uses her energies to convince herself that she is a very important person. What a heady idea to know that she can play God by forming the Brodie Set! She considers herself to be at the apex of her life, calls it her "prime," and marshals her forces to seize power over the lives of impressionable children. In the fairy-tale world in which she blazes forth as their guiding star, she feels that she is devoting her life to setting them upon the path of high achievement.

Miss Brodie appears as a supreme egotist. What she thinks, what she feels, what she pronounces—all this to her represents the truth, and she must convey this truth to others, not in a society of peers, a society in which ideas are examined, but rather in the vulnerable society of six little girls seduced by her attention to them and her constant reminding them that they are the "crème de la crème." Her attempt to make them different from the common run ranges from her introducing them to museums and her own brand of culture to hints on how to act, as well as how to deceive, when her interest is at stake. The made-up affair between her and Hugh entrances them and gives them an opportunity to vicariously experience grown-up emotions and concerns. She is, therefore, like Douglas Dougal (*The Ballad of Peckham Rye*) a Satan figure whose fatal flaw is pride. There is no arguing with her about anything. She knows it all. She is in her "prime" and must be heeded, as he is, by her set. In the final analysis, however, she is impotent, as evil must always be, according to Spark. Miss Brodie's "prime" has no lasting effect on any of her set, except perhaps Sandy. And that effect is caused because the evil of Miss Brodie has been changed to good, as Sandy becomes the epitome of goodness, a cloistered nun, a profession unacceptable to Miss Brodie. But Sandy's acceptance of her life is not clearly seen; she appears to be uncertain of her commitment as she had been uncertain of her relationship with Miss Jean Brodie.[6]

Miss Brodie, in Spark's opinion, should have been a Roman Catholic. Catholicism would have tamed the ego that rode roughshod over others' individuality and freedom. Spark infers that an ego run rampant leads to evil (as seen in Satan's downfall). The cure for this is the control inherent in the tenets of Catholicism. Once again, she is not far from Milton's thesis in *Paradise Lost*. David Lodge writes that the "world of *The Prime of Miss Jean Brodie* is a fallen world in which everybody is to some extent imperfect. . . . The true and the good are not to be found in an absolute and pure form except in God."[7] Yet Miss Brodie is also a victim, as can be seen by Spark's grouping her with the multitude of like women of her time, displaced from their ordinary role in society and forced to seek a meaningful life outside of home and family.

The counterplot, in which Sandy is the chief character, revolves around the Brodie Set and their relationship to Miss Brodie, their fascinating teacher and guide to proper behavior. Thrilled by the attention of being singled out by this actually very interesting person, they cling to her and her admonitions like bees to honey, for Miss Brodie can be sweet as she serves them tea, takes them into her confidence, and treats them as grown-ups. The little egos are flattered by the attention, and the little minds are amused by lessons that depart from the ordinary and turn the monotony of daily lessons into a never dull play. It is only Sandy who sees through the hypocrisy of Miss Brodie and finds her comic. But even she is seduced by the very real fascination of Miss Brodie and the desire to be part of her set. Miss Brodie is different from the other teachers. She is her own person, always a formidable one to encounter, completely enveloped in her own self-righteousness. No suggestion ever appears that Miss Brodie exercises any judgment on herself. To do so would jeopardize the fantasy world she inhabits and of which she makes her students a part.

To be a part of this world without the necessity of judging it gives the Brodie Set the motivation for following blindly, for the most part. Miss Brodie brings them fun, excitment, power. That she is shallow, mean, hypocritical, selfish—this is beyond the understanding of young ones who stand to lose so much should they dare to look under the facade. Sandy, who sees and does not see at the same time, remains seduced until she feels that Miss Brodie has gone "too far." Then she takes steps to put a stop to her influence. But, is Sandy's narration of events and her assessment of Miss Brodie reliable? Ruth Whittaker believes that they may not be. "Our suspicions of Sandy's motives are reinforced by the strange description of her as a nun, later in life. . . . Her betrayal of Miss Brodie has not brought her peace of mind, and her obvious agitation rather undermines our conviction of her judgment. . . . This is not to deny Miss Brodie's megalomania, but rather to suggest that Mrs. Spark's attitude to her is not as unambiguous as it first appears, and that there is implied in this novel a reluctant, conspiratorial admiration for her manipulative powers."[8]

That there is a "reluctant, conspiratorial admiration" for Miss Brodie's "manipulative powers" is not denied. The same sort of admiration appears for the Abbess of Crewe in the novel of that title. Nevertheless, although Spark appears to admire the vitality and sheer arrogance of the egocentricity of both the Abbess of Crewe and Miss Brodie, she also reveals the selfishness and the hypocrisy behind their actions. The fact that the reader may be seduced into thinking that Spark shows ambiguity in her assessment confirms the artistry of her presentation. If evil were not attractive, one would not choose it; if purveyors of evil were not fascinating, one would not follow them. If Miss Brodie had not been (and perhaps at the end of the novel still is) alluring to Sandy, she would not have chosen to follow her and to remain part of the Brodie Set. Sandy's agitation at the end might represent her ambivalence toward Miss Brodie, her uncertainty of her own course of action in betraying her. Absolutes (particularly of good and evil) do not appear in Spark's presentation of a fallen world. Absolutes belong only to God's world.

But Sandy recognizes the danger in the Brodie Set's slavish devotion to Miss Brodie. For Sandy's secret joy is going to the science laboratory. She feels that it represents freedom, because all the girls carry on their experiments by themselves. She knows that Miss Brodie's job gives her the prerogative of teaching them, but "the science class is supposed to be free, it's allowed" (38). Sandy clearly recognizes the difference. Miss Brodie's domination does not extend to the science room. Sandy's betrayal of Miss Brodie relates to her recognition of the loss of freedom engendered by the pernicious influence. The other members of the Brodie Set do not recognize this loss of freedom because they are completely enamored by the status conferred in being a member of the set. Sandy sees more clearly . Even though Sandy resents her loss of freedom under Miss Brodie, she accepts it as a nun. Although there is ambiguity in the presentation of both Miss Brodie and Sandy, the Brodie Set of which Sandy is part appears to represent goodness (they are young and innocent) and Miss Brodie appears to represent evil (she is egocentric and authoritarian). Yet innocence may not be completely good, and authoritarianism may not represent pure evil. The paradox may be seen in the final "obvious agitation" of Sandy.

Nina Auerbach calls the Marcia Blaine School for girls Spark's "most fully realized community of women" as it "attains immortality from its inextricable connection to history and time." Including it as an example of communities of women that undergird human society, Auerbach sees Jean Brodie as the "divine-demonic creation of past and coming wars" and the "personification of a city," Edinburgh.[9]

In the realm of mythology, of course, any presentation of truth may be seen as prophetic. But on a very real level, *The Prime of Miss Jean Brodie,* in its plot and counterplot, depicts the anatomy of a betrayal. When students betray teacher, it is because teacher has betrayed student. In the betrayal of God, Satan has been vanquished. In the betrayal of the good (as represented by the young girls in the Brodie Set), Miss Brodie has been vanquished. Both Satan and Miss Brodie, victims of their own monstrous pride, end with the betrayal of all that they might have become. Sandy, whose embrace of Roman Catholicism comes as a result of her love affair with Teddy Lloyd, would never have entered the convent had it not been for her teacher's influence, which turned Sandy toward a religion most abhorrent to Miss Brodie.[10] Spark appears to be saying that out of evil may come good, in that evil might be refined and tempered into good. To a believer like Spark, the tempering agent is Roman Catholicism.

Chapter Four
A Change at Midpoint

Muriel Spark's longest novel, *The Mandelbaum Gate* takes into account, for the first time in her work, contemporary events.[1] Barbara Vaughan, the protagonist, is in Israel at the time of the Eichmann Trial.[2] Spark lived in Israel for two months in 1961 in order to do research for this novel, which took her two years to write. In Israel she confronted her Jewish heritage, which she had put in the background during the time of her studying for, and her conversion to, Catholicism. *The Mandelbaum Gate,* therefore, might be considered to be her most explicitly religious novel, containing, as it does, a protagonist coming to terms with both her Jewishness and her Roman Catholicism, a task necessary for Spark herself.

In 1962, Mrs. Spark moved to America, where she lived for three years, loving New York's activity and using the office given to her by the *New Yorker* magazine. She began the novel *The Hothouse by the East River* there, but it was not published until 1973.

Becoming disillusioned with America, she moved to Rome in 1966, where she lives in a large apartment overlooking the Tiber. This resulted in a shift in emphasis in her plots toward contemporary happenings, particularly robbery, kidnapping, spying, and treachery of all sorts. She "admits her fascination with the Italian popular press, which furnishes her ideas for plots: 'The journalists here are more imaginative than any I know. A combination of Latin blood and a free press. . . . I think a lot of their energy, which might have gone into novel writing, goes into their reporting.' "[3]

In a telephone interview in 1983, Spark states that she really lives "in the country, in Tuscany, with a friend who has a house there." She states, "I have a place in Rome, but I only come here to have a little social life, answer letters, things like that. I usually write in the country. But I do go to France and Germany quite a lot and to England, of course, and to the United States quite often."[4]

The Mandelbaum Gate, The Abbess of Crewe, and *Territorial Rights* include secular and contemporary problems that reflect humans' distortion of God's image into their own. This theme is seen in the distortion of

truth through language, the absurdity of current events, and the problem
of survival in the face of threats both political and domestic.

The Mandelbaum Gate

Like Muriel Spark, Barbara Vaughan, the protagonist of *The Mandelbaum Gate* (1965) is half-Jewish and half-English and has become
a convert to Roman Catholicism. Barbara feels a "compelling need to
find some definition that would accurately explain herself to this man,"[5]
"this man" being her guide in Israel. Her attempt to find this definition
compels her to visit the shrines of Jordan, separated from Israel by the
Mandelbaum Gate, through which she is not allowed to pass because
of her Jewish ancestry. Her successful completion of her visit to Jordan
and her finding the desired definition form the basis of the novel. The
novel also concerns Freddy Hamilton, age fifty, employee of the British
consulate in Israel's Jerusalem and his propulsion into Barbara's quest.
As he helps her, he gains in courage himself. He also serves as an
observer of the absurdity of the situation surrounding the enemy factions
of Israel and Jordan.

As in the other novels, time in *The Mandelbaum Gate* swings between
past and present. It opens with Freddy Hamilton, who somewhat
resembles Ronald Bridges, the epileptic in *The Bachelors,* a nice person,
meek and mild, a bachelor to all intents, having been but briefly
married at a young age. With an innate innocence, he sees the entire
situation pictured in the novel as "absurd," starting with the "quite
absurd" Mandelbaum Gate (6). The basic absurdity becomes readily
apparent as Freddy notices that "the Orthodox Jews would gather on
a Saturday morning, piously to stone the passing motor cars, breakers
of the Sabbath" (7).

Into Freddy's humdrum life comes Barbara Vaughan, a schoolteacher
from England about to visit her fiancé Harry Clegg, an archeologist
digging in Jordan. Although Barbara and Harry have been having an
affair and Barbara feels no guilt about it, she wishes Harry to get an
annulment of his previous marriage in order that they might marry in
the church. Yet, she will marry him without the annulment, even
though she worries about the uneasiness of her future life should she
do so. Meanwhile, she has become reconciled with the church, repenting
of her adultery, although she feels that "it is impossible to repent of
love. The sin does not exist" (51). Thus Barbara, as can be seen by

this curious reasoning, indicates that she is mixed up about more than her Jewish-English heritage.

To visit the Christian shrines in Jordan, Barbara must pass through the Mandelbaum Gate by showing her baptismal certificate and by hiding the fact that she is half-Jewish. Her Jewish ancestry, if known, would make her suspect as a spy, enemy of the Arabs. Freddy does not wish to be involved in Barbara's predicament because he is afraid that she has "some tiresome deep conviction" (17). At this point Freddy has no convictions. But Barbara notes his morally feeble nature and quotes a passage from the Book of the Apocalypse that she says applies to his point of view: "I know thy doings, and find thee neither cold nor hot; cold or hot, I would thou wert one or the other. Being what thou art, lukewarm, neither cold nor hot, thou wilt make me vomit thee out of my mouth!" (17). Although Freddy finds this quoting of the Scriptures "quite absurd," it remains in his memory and motivates him to action. In fact, he himself quotes it later.

But Freddy must overcome his fear of involvement. Freddy travels freely between Israel and Jordan, and on a visit to Matt and Joanna, his friends in Jordan, he mentions Barbara's desire to visit Jordan. Matt indicates that not only would she be in trouble but they would all be in trouble, because the "government here is looking for a bit of trouble with the Jews at the moment" (76). Freddy becomes afraid that he might be involved in an international incident. He feels that he must do something to keep her from going to Jordan. And when Matt suggests that Freddy take away her passport, he replies, "Oh, no. . . . she's nothing to do with us," but he "did not like the sound of his words as they were the sort of words that always, to the outsider, suggested Pontious [sic] Pilate washing his hands of a potential source of embarrassment." But Freddy feels sympathy for Pilate and for all who "like himself, no doubt, had been officially dim, dutiful, and absolutely against intervention between individuals and their doom" (80–81).

Thus Freddy, although fearful of making a commitment to help Barbara, realizes that there is betrayal in the idea of keeping oneself from what might become embarrassing, if not dangerous. This understanding results in his feeling protective toward Barbara when he meets her unexpectedly in a shop in Jordan. Barbara had come through the Mandelbaum Gate by using her extra passport, one that does not show the Israeli visa. The feeling of protectiveness leads to his change from timidity to commitment. He tells Matt, "The trouble with you . . .

is that you blow neither hot nor cold, but lukewarm . . . and I will spew thee out of my mouth. . . . Very apt" (89–90). Barbara's quotation from Apocalypse thus seems to be the catalyst that forces Freddy into a contemplation of his wishy-washy nature, with the result that he becomes a person of commitment.

Freddy's commitment consists of helping Barbara to get safely back to Israel after she has visited the desired shrines. This task becomes dangerous, because everything becomes known in this land of intrigue, including the fact that Barbara is half-Jewish. The absurdity of the consideration of Barbara as a possible spy is pointed up by the fact that Joe Ramdez, an Arab living in Jordan, and Abdul, his son living in Israel, together carry on intrigue for both sides, never doing any real harm and at the same time doing themselves much financial good. In a further absurdity, Suzi Ramdez, Abdul's sister, and Freddy succeed in getting Barbara safely returned to Israel by disguising her as an old Arab woman and then as a nun, stealing the clothes from a visiting tourist nun, leaving her naked.

Freddy's courageous commitment to Barbara allows him to participate in catching a spy, the wife of his colleague. Ruth Gardner (the spy) has been using what is called "Nasser's Post Office," a slit in the bark of the tree at the home of Joe Ramdez, where Barbara is recovering from a slight case of scarlet fever, preparatory for her return to Israel. Freddy discovers Ruth and is able to implicate his colleague although, again absurdly, she escapes. The trauma of Freddy's courageous acts apparently are too much for his ordinary, weak nature, and he loses his memory for a few days, but it comes back in time for him to reveal the whereabouts and the users of "Nasser's Post Office." Therefore, Freddy's ability to transcend his cautious nature in order to help Barbara brings him the unexpected reward of being able to do something for his country.

The absurdity of Barbara and Harry marrying in the church, despite the fact that Harry remains married to his former wife comes about because Ricky, the former headmistress of the school Barbara taught at, who wishes to prevent Barbara's marriage, forges a baptismal certificate for Harry. She erroneously believes that if she can show him to have been baptized a Catholic, he will not be able to marry Barbara in the church. But her plan backfires, setting him free to marry Barbara, his first marriage having been declared invalid as one between a Catholic and a non-Catholic. Ricky herself becomes the third wife of Joe Ramdez, the Arab blackmailer who keeps prostitutes for the use of English diplomats and civil servants and then blackmails his clients by forcing them to buy shares in his nonexistent insurance company.

The absurdity of the entire situation the characters find themselves in (and Freddy constantly points this out) is demonstrated at the end when Freddy, walking around the city, comes to the Mandelbaum Gate and recognizes that it is "hardly a gate at all, but a piece of street between Jerusalem and Jerusalem, flanked by two huts, and called by that name because a house at the other end once belonged to a Mr. Mandelbaum" (369). The irrationality of political life, particularly the enmity between Israel and Jordan, pervades the novel. Freddy sees all things as absurd, and from the God's-eye view presented by Muriel Spark, all things are. Barbara, the Catholic convert, also acts inconsistently in her giving up of the sexual relationship with Harry in order to be reconciled to the church, yet admitting she will marry him anyway, even without an annulment, and then marrying him, knowing that the letter of the law has not been served. The foolishness of Ricky's action in obtaining the false baptismal certificate results in the very act she wishes to prevent.

Although the enmity between Israel and Jordan is pointed to constantly, each side suspicious of the other, Joe Ramdez in Jordan and his son Abdul in Israel continually engage in intrigue, not through conviction of a political stance, but purely for their own gain. Abdul, who gives lessons in Arabic to Freddy, feels "mentally closer" to Freddy than he does to his father (102). This is not surprising, as Freddy is a much more attractive person than Joe Ramdez, and Abdul is an attractive young man. But the absurdity of adhering to one political side or the other becomes clear when Abdul puts Freddy in the category of those who belong to the "System," which includes "their fathers, the Pope, President Nasser, King Hussein, Mr. Ben-Gurion, the Grand Mufti, the Patriarch of Jerusalem, the English Sovereign, the civil servants and upper militia throughout the world, and all the other representatives of the police forces of life who, however beneficent, had absentmindedly put his generation as a whole in difficulties." He has decided that it was best "to mix up his elders as to his motives, to defeat and exasperate them by transparent guile and hypocrisy, to have no motives at all, but to be enchanting throughout his days" (92–93).

And both Abdul and his sister Suzi are enchanting, attractive young people who act helpfully and gracefully in getting Barbara safely back to Israel. They refuse to be drawn into a commitment to a foolish

political division, a division possible because those involved refuse to
face reality honestly.

Even though Freddy recognizes the absurdity of the social and political
structure, he does not have an understanding of the falsity of the various
commitments, the understanding Abdul has. Conservative by nature,
Freddy represents the good civil servant, good at obeying orders and
not straying far from the accepted norm. It is only when faced with
the necessity of helping Barbara that the dormant idea laid by her
remark about his lukewarmness heats him up sufficiently to goad him
into becoming a different person. And then, as if to blot out the horror
of his aggression, he loses memory of the actions he courageously took.

Furthur absurdity manifests itself when Ricky, on a trip to prevent
Barbara's marriage, ends up in bed with Joe Ramdez, who already has
a wife, and later actually marries him. The presentation of the correct
headmistress becoming what amounts to the concubine of the lusty
Arab, blackmailer and keeper of prostitutes, provides much comedy
under Spark's deft pen. The absurdity of Ricky's providing the means
of a solemnized marriage for Barbara when she believed that she was
doing the exact opposite has already been pointed out. And Joe Ramdez
actually loves Ricky—and she him—the height of the absurd.

For Barbara Vaughan, traveling to gain a sense of herself, the trip
is enlightening, much as her own trip must have been for Barbara's
creator, Muriel Spark. Both were searching for their roots. Barbara's
"habits of mind were inadequate to cope with the whole of her
experience," and so she "was in a state of conflict, like practically
everyone else in some mode or another . . . and she was one of those
afflicted by her gifts. For she was gifted with an honest, analytical
intelligence, a sense of fidelity in the observing of observable things,
and at the same time, with the beautiful and dangerous gift of faith
which, by definition of the Scriptures, is the sum of things hoped for
and the evidence of things unseen" (20). It is easy to see Muriel Spark
in this description.

Barbara's faith is indeed dangerous, literally and figuratively. Literally,
her being half-Jewish makes her suspect in Jordan as a spy. Figuratively,
her faith presents a danger to her identity as a person, since she must
circumvent the literal teaching of the letter of the law given by her
church in order to achieve freedom of will. The absurdity of the situation
inherent in the Mandelbaum Gate manifests itself in her gaining free
access to Jordan, where she is suspect because of her Jewish blood and

not wanted, and the necessity of her escaping disguised as a nun to Israel, where her Jewish blood gains her a welcome.

Barbara's growth reveals itself in the complexity surrounding motivation in the novel. Certainly the mixed-up motives of the belligerents on both sides of the Israel-Jordan border reveal an absurdity that can only be understood by attributing to each person either an inherited course of action, engaged in without thought, or one engaged in for purely selfish reasons. For Freddy, it was to do the "right thing." For Abdul Ramdez, it was to do what confused, in order to punish the system. For Joe Ramdez, it was to do what would bring him the most money: providing prostitutes, engaging in blackmail, marrying an Englishwoman he thinks is rich.

Barbara feels that Ricky was "all for doing the right thing for the right reason; she was fierce—principled about motives." But for Barbara, "one of the first attractions of her religion's moral philosophy had been its recognition of the helpless complexity of motives that prompted an action, and its consequent emphasis on actual words, thoughts and deeds; there was seldom one motive only in a grown person; the main thing was that motives should harmonize" (190). The wholeness of the person seems to be, for Barbara, the harmonizing of one's motives, acting maturely according to one's principles. An affirmation of the spirit rather than the letter of the law enables one to effect this harmony. This affirmation is reflected in Barbara's relaxed response to the strict dictates of her newfound Catholic religion.

Lying on the camp bed at an old monk's retreat during her escape from Jordan, "for the first time since her arrival in the Middle East she felt all of a piece: Gentile and Jewess, Vaughan and Aaronson." She feels that she has "caught some of Freddy's madness," feeling, that, like him, she has come from ancestors who were "unself-questioning hierarchists, anarchistic imperialists, blood-sporting zoophiles, sceptical believers—the whole paradoxical lark that had secured, among their bones, the sane life for the dead generations of British Islanders. . . . For the first time in this Holy Land, [she] felt all of a piece, a Gentile Jewess, a private-judging Catholic, a shy adventuress" (194). At this point, Barbara may be said to have "found herself," knowing now what she stands for, proud of her heritage, mixed though it is, recognizing the part that each ancestor, orthodox or unorthodox, has played in helping to form her. As the necessity of helping Barbara to escape has liberated Freddy from the stifling rules he has lived under, Freddy's "madness" in planning and carrying out her escape has liberated Barbara from the fragmentation she formerly felt as the product of a divided heritage.

Freddy has been living under rules that he failed to examine. He uses language to distort the truth. At the opening of the novel, the reader learns that he compiles verses when he wishes to thank his hostess for a pleasant stay. He feels himself a boring person, and this practice represents an attempt to make himself agreeable. Avoiding emotion, he can distort feeling through the triviality of his atrocious rhymes. He has also accepted the lies of his tyrant mother, which can "only with difficulty be denounced because of her long-sustained tyranny." Conversely, her "tyranny could hardly now be overthrown because of her long-condoned lies" (66). It is only when Freddy decides to help Barbara escape from Jordan that he rejects the lies. He burns a letter he has written to his mother and flushes it down the toilet. It is his gesture of freedom both from the tyranny of his mother and from the tyranny of rules never examined.

After he succeeds in spiriting Barbara from the convent she has sought refuge in and spends almost three days helping her back to Israel, he reflects on his adventure and is "amazed." The adventure "had seemed to transfigure his life, without any disastrous change in the appearance of things; pleasantly and essentially he came to feel it had made a free man of him where before he had been the subdued, obedient servant of a mere disorderly sensation, that of impersonal guilt. And whether this feeling of Freddy's subsequent years was justified or not, it did him good to harbour it" (165–66). Spark allows her character to finish his own story.

Freddy not only makes himself free (at least for the duration of Barbara's escape) but he affects Barbara's determination to continue with the pilgrimage and not seek refuge in the embassy. He challenges her to dare her freedom at the same time that he is daring his. She tells Harry later that she continued with the pilgrimage because Freddy wanted her to be "a good sport." Harry asks her just what is the technical Catholic difference between being a martyr and a "jolly good sport," implying in the question, of course, that there is no difference.

Later, when Barbara finds out that Freddy has suffered from amnesia, which wiped out all memory of the escape, she is "shocked" that "so much of that carefree and full-hearted Freddy had turned sour with guilt" (198). Freddy's change of perspective, therefore, is left ambiguous. He does not take steps to find out whether Suzi Ramdez is still alive, fearing that the search would reveal that she is dead. This appears to indicate that Freddy still avoids emotion, still lacks courage to face the truth, lest it be unpleasant. But for a period of a few days, at least, he acted in daring freedom. Both Barbara and Freddy break their rigid code, but Barbara's new insight lasts. One critic remarks, "From limited sensibility, unable to encompass important aspects of her experience, Barbara approaches the unity of being frequently sought but rarely found" by Spark's characters. "In Eichmann, and in her own darker nature, she sees a void beyond conventional moralities, a void that forces man to encounter experience without props, to realize there is no code that relieves him of the burdens of choice."[6] For Barbara (and for Spark) mindless obedience, as exemplified by the defendants in the Nuremburg Trials and by Adolf Eichmann, tried in Israel in 1961 for Nazi atrocities, must not be the norm of behavior, and this means even mindless obedience to the church.

The problem of survival finds a solution by either being a good sport and doing the right thing like Freddy and Barbara, or by refusing to pretend that absurdity is rationality; thus Abdul and his father engage in lies and chicanery, playing both sides against the middle but believing in neither. Barbara can accomplish her goal of pilgrimage to the holy land in Jordan because she lives up to Freddy's definition of "good sport." Freddy can survive the very real danger of being caught and shot as a spy while helping Barbara because he is the "good sport" who dares to put his freedom on the line.

An irrational world, in which religion becomes a stepping stone to power, spawns survivors who, bereft of illusions as to the morality of their actions, feed on the suspicions of factions whose positions have been inherited, are deep-seated, and who fail to realize the cause of the enmity between them or to recognize the absurdity of it. The world has fallen from God's creative foundation. Godless, its inhabitants absurdly pursue form without substance, design without God's limiting grace.

Warner Berthoff writes that Muriel Spark "writes about satisfaction, Iris Murdoch writes about love." He says that in *The Mandelbaum Gate,* "all are satisfied within the course plotted for them; all get their due and are provided for." He also takes issue with the novel because "instead of a graspable action of love, faith, participation in destiny, Muriel Spark gives us her sharp, definite, restrictive idea about these things and about the effect their presence or absence has upon individual men and women."[7] But the beauty of her creation lies precisely in delineating the effect of the absence of such things as "love, faith, participation in destiny."

Sibyl Bedford finds that this novel leaves one with an "afterglow. Instead of being asked to remember that we must die (as in *Memento Mori*), we are asked to remember that we should live."[8] Barbara "lives" because she has dared to make herself whole; Freddy "lives" (if only for a time), because he has dared to be brave. But the world that surrounds them, absurd in its Godlessness, has ceased to follow the pattern of its Divine Maker and suffers the consequences of chaos.

The Abbess of Crewe

Spark's movement away from the religious into the secular and the contemporary can be clearly seen in *The Abbess of Crewe* (1974). Although set in an abbey with the main character an abbess, it is not religious in nature but rather a satire on the use of religion to obtain power as well as a satire on the reforms of the Catholic church. It focuses on contemporary problems that extend into the supposedly godly and serene life of an abbey. The main problem concerns an election, complete with bugging devices and other chicanery; the novel is a delightful, witty, extraordinarily perceptive parody of the Watergate scandal.[9] Its light-hearted tone and cynically shrewd cunning place the characters on an objective plane, so that the reader can enjoy and applaud without sitting in judgment on the evil actions below the surface.

The plot is a simple one. The abbey is faced with a scandal concerning activities described by Sister Felicity who has left the abbey in the company of her Jesuit lover. Flashbacks reveal the start of the action that culminates in Felicity's departure.

Felicity, who attempts to instill the young sisters with ideas of love and freedom, is a contender for the position of abbess against Alexandra, who cannot bear even the thought of losing the election. In order to circumvent Felicity's attraction for the young sisters, who have a vote in the election, Alexandra enlists the aid of a Jesuit friend who sends two young Jesuit novices to raid Sister Felicity's sewing basket in search of incriminating love letters, with which Alexandra hopes to discredit her. In their zeal, the young Jesuits take, or misplace, Felicity's silver thimble, the loss of which reveals that a robbery has taken place. The tug between Felicity and Alexandra for the position of abbess ends with Felicity's escape from the convent and Alexandra's installation as Abbess of Crewe. As abbess, she must quiet the scandal started by Felicity's revelation of the burglary. Before leaving for Rome "to respond to the Congregational Committee of Investigation into the case of Sister Felicity's little thimble and thimble-related matters,"[10] she gives orders to have tape recordings of her prayers transcribed. She tells the nuns to put "poetry deleted" at the places where she has recited secular verse instead of religious liturgy.[11] The deletions, as on the Watergate tapes, signify the removal of emotional outbursts.

The novel opens with the abbess and Sister Winifrede walking along a path lined with poplars, discussing the bugging of the abbey, which the authorities are closely watching in view of the recent scandal. The abbess is a "very Lombardy poplar" with a face that is "a white-skinned English skull, beautiful in the frame of her white nun's coif." At age forty-two she has "fourteen generations of pale and ruling ancestors of England, and ten before them of France, carved . . . into the bones of her wonderful head" (1–2).

The authoritarian character of the abbess reveals itself immediately in her arrogance. Like Miss Brodie, Alexandra, Abbess of Crewe, is a rule unto herself, imperious and self-seeking. She admits to Winifrede that she has bugged the poplars under which they walk, that it is the only way they can operate in the face of the scandal. She warns Winifrede, "And now that you know this you do not know it so to speak. We have our security to consider. . . . I'm your conscience and your authority. You perform my will" (3). Distortion of truth and blind obedience to the abbess's will must be Winifrede's lot.

The convent itself is a mixture of the old and the new: "distant in its newness from all the orthodoxies of the past . . . far removed in its antiquities from those of the present! 'It's the only way,' she once said, this Alexandra, the noble Lady Abbess, 'to find an answer always ready to hand for any adverse criticism whatsoever.' " And she admits that "there is nothing at all on paper to reveal the mighty pact between the Abbey of Crewe and the Jesuit hierarchy, the overriding and most profitable pact. What Jesuits know of it but the few?" (4).

And yet both nuns and monks of the Benedictine order, the order of the Abbey of Crewe, knowing of the abbess's insistence on the ancient rule and refusal of the reforms of the Vatican Council, "marvelled that such a great and so Benedictine a lady should have brought her strictly enclosed establishment to the point of an international newspaper scandal" (4–5). Thus Alexandra's goal is to rule with an iron hand, keeping the convent free of criticism, while she lives outwardly the pious nun.

In keeping with the "only way" of avoiding adverse criticism, the past rule of reading at meals is followed. But the readings are not only from the Rule of Benedict; they are also from a book on electronic transmission. The ancient custom of getting up at three in the morning for prayers is followed, but the abbess intersperses the words of the psalms with her own more sensuous ones. Further, the ancient custom of bringing a dowry is followed, but the great fortunes brought to the convent include "a sizeable block of Chicago slums" and "a section of Park Lane with its view of Rotten Row" in London (31–32). The Park Lane property is among the most expensive in London. The paradox of the religious women holding expensive property and also being slumlords underscores the hypocrisy of the lives they live: outwardly pious, inwardly evil.

Alexandra herself did not bring a dowry to the community, except "her noble birth and shrewd spirit" (33). They are formidable gifts, however. Her nobility gives her the ruthlessness necessary to rule, and her shrewd spirit enables her to excel in the hypocrisy that her authoritarian nature demands. There is a hint that Sister Hildegarde, the late abbess, has been her lover.

At three in the morning, while the nuns are chanting Lauds, "the Abbess from her high seat looks with a kind of wonder at her shadowy chapel of nuns, she listens with a fine joy to the keen plainchant, as if upon a certain newly created world. She contemplates and sees it is good. Her lips move with the Latin of the psalm. She stands before her high chair as one exalted by what she sees and thinks, as it might be she is contemplating the full existence of the Abbess of Crewe" (26). Presented as God, secure in her knowledge that her throne must not topple, instead of singing the Latin of the psalm, she whispers "the melodious responses in other words of her great liking":

> Every farthing of the cost,
> All the dreaded cards foretell,
> Shall be paid, but from this night
> Not a whisper, not a thought,
> Not a kiss nor look be lost. (26–27)

Although Sister Felicity, according to Alexandra, is "too timid to hate well, let alone love" (29), she has the courage to meet her Jesuit lover in the middle of the night. She also has the courage to flee and to live with him, while going to the authorities about the bugging and other atrocities at the abbey, including the serving of dog and cat food to the nuns while the rulers of the abbey and their friends dine on delicacies. Felicity appears to be a rather good, if naive person, a humanist. In Alexandra's opinion she "claims a special enlightenment . . . wants everyone to be liberated by her vision and to acknowledge it. She wants a stamped receipt from Almighty God for every word she spends, every action, as if she can later deduct it from her income-tax returns. Felicity will never see the point of faith unless it visibly benefits mankind." Sister Walburga, the novice-mistress agrees that Felicity is "so bent on helping lame dogs over stiles. . . . Then they can't get back over again to limp home." Sister Mildred adds that Felicity is likewise "helping Thomas" who had "offered to help" Mildred (34). This "helping" refers to the sexual relationship Thomas the Jesuit wished first to establish with Mildred, but when she refused established with Felicity. The ruling nuns clearly have no love for Felicity.

But Felicity, enjoying her forbidden sexual freedom, wants others to be happy as well. Unrestrained in carnal appetite and do-gooder though she appears, she stands as the complete opposite of Alexandra. For Felicity, the world runs on love and freedom; for Alexandra, it runs on greed and oppression.

If Alexandra and Felicity represent opposite poles, Sister Gertrude, the globe-trotting Kissinger, represents the pragmatic middle. Both Alexandra and Felicity communicate with her on the "Green Line," radio transmissions that connect them to the most remote regions of the globe. Both Alexandra and Felicity call her to ask for help, and she advises them pragmatically, at the same time indicating her own exotic activities. Alexandra attempts to get her to come back to help her win the election, but Gertrude cannot leave because she is negotiating between a cannibal tribe and a vegetarian sect. Alexandra urges her to leave the cannibals alone because of the problem of identifying them on Resurrection Day: "those that are eaten having long since become the consumers from generation to generation" (42–43). But Gertrude is not listening because she is busy tying her shoelace.

Alexandra, trying another argument, tries to convince Gertrude that it is immoral for Felicity to run for abbess, even though she has a chance. Gertrude replies that "a rebellion against a tyrant is only immoral when it hasn't got a chance" (43–44). Gertrude, cynic though she is and purportedly helping Alexandra, recognizes the tyrant that Alexandra is. She advises Alexandra to consult Machiavelli's "Art of War" (which Alexandra does). At the end, when Alexandra confers with Gertrude as to how to respond when Rome asks why they adhere to the old yet follow the new, Gertrude says it is not a problem, only a paradox, and "a paradox you live with" (22). Writing to Rome, Alexandra remembers this, and master of the language of duplicity, explains that "religion is founded on principles of Paradox. . . . Paradox is to be accepted and presents no problem. . . . electronic surveillance (even if a convent were one day to practise it) does not differ from any other type of watchfulness, the which is a necessity of a Religious Community; we are told in the Scriptures 'to watch and to pray', which is itself a paradox since the two activities cannot effectively be practised together except in the paradoxical sense." Then she asks the nuns if they think what she has written will "succeed in getting them muddled up for awhile" (24).

When Felicity secretly calls Gertrude to enlist her help because the convent is a "hotbed of corruption and hypocrisy," that she wants to make changes, "break free," secure "justice," Gertrude replies with her usual cynicism. "Justice may be done but on no account should it be seen to be done. It's always a fatal undertaking. You'll bring down the whole community in ruins" (49–50).

But the pragmatic Gertrude has not helped Felicity to win the election, as Alexandra has convinced the young nuns, snobs all, that the choice is between nobility and bourgeoisie, she, of course being nobility. Blackmailed by the young Jesuits who broke in and later by the novice nuns, Alexandra reveals nevertheless that she never worries, an indication of the tremendous confidence she has in her ability to get out of serious predicaments. The nuns excuse their implication in the scandal by saying that they had to have Alexandra win. Now they must think of some scenarios, which Alexandra defines as "an art form based on facts. A good scenario is a garble. A bad one is a bungle. They need not be plausible, only hypnotic, like all good art!" (95). The parody of Watergate cannot be more clear.

Gertrude (the globe-trotting Kissinger) apparently plays the role of Conscience, yet remains cynically aware of reality. She tells Alexandra that she should not have pried, should have invested the dowries for the good of the convent, and should have stopped the break-in. She says, "I am outraged . . . to hear you have all been sinning away there at Crewe, and exceedingly at that, not only in thought and deed but also in word. I have been toiling and spinning while, if that sensational text is to be believed, you have been considering the lilies and sinning exceedingly. You are at fault, all of you, most grievously at fault" (114). And it is Gertrude who tells Alexandra to delete the English poetry from the tapes, when Alexandra says, "In response to popular demand . . . I have decided to make selected transcripts of my tapes and publish them. I find some passages are missing and fear that the devil who goes about as a raging lion hath devoured them. There are many film and stage offers, and all these events will help tremendously to further your work in the field and to assist the starved multitudes. Gertrude you know I have become an object of art, the end of which is to give pleasure!" (113). The abbess shows herself, indeed, as a master of rhetoric. Her phrases from the Bible become the facade housing her hypocrisy.

And she has become an object of art,[12] and reading her story does give pleasure. It is impossible to record the wit, the humor, and the delightful twists of language that make this novel one of Spark's funniest and most entertaining. The distortion of truth through language by the Abbess of Crewe parallels in hilarious detail the distortion of truth heard in Watergate. The comic irony of a contemporary event placed in the context of a religious community is irreverent, but provides basic insight and brings to the reader a sense of its innate outrage as well as its humor, revealing the author's genius.

Territorial Rights

Continuing with an emphasis on contemporary problems, in *Territorial Rights* (1979) Spark focuses on the invasion of the space around the individual by the blackmailer, or to a lesser extent, by the snooper who implies blackmail. The comic-tragic nature of events of this novel reflect the comic-tragic events of the contemporary world, a world that, according to Spark, has lost the ability to see itself as absurd. While not specifically comparing this fallen world to the divine one, she presents the characters in ridiculous situations, with the result that the novel becomes in part a black comedy. The reader enjoys the comedy of evil characters enmeshed in the ridiculous actions they take in order to survive. Overall, the author remains objective, allowing the ludicrous nature of the events to speak for themselves.

Robert Leaver, a thoroughly dislikable young man, is in Venice, having left his rich, sophisticated, lover-protector, Mark Curran. He meets a former acquaintance, Lina Pancev, who has come to Italy to find the grave of her father, a political activist from Bulgaria who had escaped to Italy many years before. Also in Vienna is Robert's father,

Arnold Leaver, on a vacation with his mistress Mary Tiller, who formerly taught cooking at Ambrose, the school Robert attended and at which his father was headmaster. Also arriving is Grace Gregory, former matron at Robert's school, who is in Vienna on behalf of Robert's mother, Anthea, who suspects her husband of philandering. Grace tells Leo, the young man who accompanies her, that she "used to keep Arnold temperate . . . in the sick-bay when there were no boys sick."[13] Thus are his wife's suspicions deftly confirmed.

Into this company comes Violet de Winter, chief agent for the Global-Equipt Security Services for Northern Italy, part of the concern to which Anthea has gone to get help in spying on her husband. Violet, a longtime friend of Mark Curran, meets him in Vienna, to which he has come to settle things once and for all with Robert. The Global concern is, in reality, a blackmailing organization that preys on rich people in the guise of helping them. Two sisters, Eufenia and Katerina, run the Pensione Sofia, the hotel at which Robert stays.

This motley mix serves as characters in a rather slow-moving, complicated, but deftly handled story, in which Lina unknowingly dances on her father's grave and returns to Bulgaria with her cousin Serge, where she is "put to happy use as a first-rate example of a repentant dissident" (238). Her account of her stay in Vienna shows her erroneous perception of events and reveals as well the complicated nature of the story line.

Lina describes her "tumble-down flat . . . [in the home of] the slave-driving countess who forbade her to eat meat." This countess is Viola, who employed Lina and forbade her to patronize the butcher, because he has blackmailed all concerned about the disposition of Lina's father's body. The body was cut in two by the butcher's father (witnessed by him) and buried in the rose garden of the Pensione Sofia, one half on each side, so that the garden could be tended individually by the two who loved him and fought for his body. Mark Curran and Viola, although not involved in the death of Lina's father, were connected with the Axis powers, spying for them, a fact they do not wish to have revealed. Lina, also, as the "repentant dissident" still cries over the fact that she never found her father's grave (although she unknowingly danced on it, courtesy of Robert, apparently his idea of humor). Lina also tells of "the elderly American millionaire who went about with a briefcase full of dollars seducing young people of both sexes" (238–39)— a reference to Curran's pay-off to the butcher. Lina, believing that

Curran had forgotten the satchetful of cash he had left for the pay-off, ran after him with it.

Further complicating the plot, Robert becomes friends with the butcher Giorgio and his niece Anna, thereby learning of the buried body. He keeps notes and leaves them where they will be found, adding to the fright of all involved, particularly Curran and Viola. He adds unsavory bits about Mary Tiller and Grace Gregory to these notes also. Robert and Anna rob a bank, kill a customer and a policeman, and are called "Bonnie and Clyde" by the newspapers. While the two are having a drink in Trieste, they are spotted by a "talent spotter" who knows about their daring crime and tells them, "You've got style. You can make it to the top." As a result they are "sent to the Middle East to train in a terrorist camp" (238).

When Robert sends his mother a very valuable diamond and sapphire bracelet with a letter that he is a traveling executive, she is delighted, never dreaming that the bracelet is stolen. Arnold returns, at the end, to his wife Anthea, while his former mistresses Mary Tiller and Grace Gregory take a world tour together, Mary feeling agreeably guilty and Grace agreeably innocent about their past life. Grace strikes Spark's cynical note when she tells Anthea, "You're mistaken if you think wrongdoers are always unhappy. The really professional evil-doers love it. . . . The unhappy ones are only the guilty amateurs and the neurotics" (235). Grace, through her experience as school matron, has learned the ways of the wicked ones. And her words appear true, especially as applied to Robert.

The other characters do not fare badly either. Curran goes to India to see his guru after paying the butcher the blackmail money. Violet persuades Leo (Grace's young friend) to join her in a tourist project, "Venice by Night," which turns out to be a prosperous undertaking, not likely the result of strictly legal activity. Katerina and Eufenia remain busy in the Pensione Sofia, each cultivating the part of the rose garden under which her part of Lina's father's body lies, and "the mosaics stood with the same patience that had gone into their formation, piece by small piece" (240).

This last sentence of the novel gives a clue to the basic theme. The mosaic, put together piece by small piece, has remained a whole, just as the mosaic of the lives involved has remained a whole despite the threat to it. The huge blackmail payment made by Curran to the butcher has allowed the mosaic of secrets to remain. The fallen world has reached a point in which crime operates freely and blackmail payments prevent the truth from being revealed. No longer does Spark contrast the divine purpose with the activities of those who thwart that purpose. "In fact her work almost ceases to be comparative at all, very nearly becoming a statement of absolute fact about a fallen and godless world."[14]

In the end, then, things are what they were before: Arnold is home once more with Anthea, Lina is back in Bulgaria, Violet is again scheming, Curran is off to his guru, Katerina and Eufenia run the Pensione Sofia and tend their graves, Grace Gregory and Mary Tiller, pleasant if not forceful characters, end up having a good time together. Robert has become the criminal his schoolboy invasion of the "territorial rights" of others promised, when he snooped in Grace Gregory's room. His prying uncovered the entire story of Lina's father. "I snooped," he says, "I got information" (217).

The message of the novel is not murder-will-out; rather, the cover-up succeeds. Through a complicated maneuvering of plot and character, Spark succeeds in drawing all the skeins together with deftness and, as is characteristic, many wry and cynical comments on people and their ways. Satirizing the rebels against capitalistic society in her portraits of Lina and Serge, she holds them up as likable, even though they are ridiculous in their conclusions, as indicated by Lina's summary of her sojourn in Vienna.

Robert, the most unpleasant character, an inveterate snoop, is the prime invader of independent space. From the time he looks for what might tell him unpleasant facts about others, rummaging in Grace Gregory's belongings at school, until he leaves his notes about the burial of Lina's father where those involved will see them, he invades the space of others for his own ends. Grace says, "Give people a story and they believe it, especially if there are one or two authentic facts and dates" (154). She is referring to notes found about her. Robert has written, "Grace Gregory, a former nightclub stripper of (c.) 1930 AD, at the height of the bourgeois-fascist London ethos, later contracts a marriage with one Gregory who has a license to run a public house in Norfolk" (152). Grace explains that actually she "used to do a dance-turn" but she would not "call it strip" (153). There is much more that Robert has included in his notes on her past life, all hyperbolized to make her past appear lurid.

His father notes that Robert is "capable of anything" (47), which appears literally true as Robert ends up that hardest of all criminals, a terrorist. Curran admits to Violet that Robert "is not a very nice

young man. Rather nasty, in fact" (89). Mary Tiller, who also appears
in Robert's notes as "a middle-aged fascist-bourgeois woman poisoner
whose three husbands. . . ." (151), says that she does not believe
Robert is mad, but that "he might be evil" (177).

Curran admits to his lawyer that when he met Robert, the latter
was in Paris posing as a student but in reality operating as a prostitute.
Robert pursues his own interests by invading the "territorial rights" of
others, which include the right to privacy. He ends up as a product
of his own misdeeds. Having helped to provide the facts that resulted
in the blackmail payment and having masterminded, with Anna, the
bank robbery, he becomes the evil person outside all law, the terrorist.
Like Dougal *(The Ballad of Peckham Rye)* Robert has used real facts
about the past of individuals to harass them and cause mischief. But
Robert actually embellishes the facts deliberately for blackmail purposes,
where Dougal allowed the individuals' own guilty conscience to do the
job for him.

Lina Pancev hovers between goodness, naiveté, and stupidity. She is
the parody of a dissident. In a letter from a woman friend in the
radical movement Lina reads: "The Group feels this way. Don't be
upset, Lina but you know you never answer letters, sign petitions or
come to our meetings and our demonstrations. Additional to this, there
has been a report that you are not seriously a Dissident. Isn't it true,
Lina, that you believe in nothing and know nothing of our struggle?
Please do not take this personally, but you should never have left
Bulgaria. Nobody was persecuting you. You do not suffer. You do not
share our aims. Many stories have been spread about you. Your ideas.
. . ." (181). And Lina fits the description. She has become a dissident
because it is fashionable, apparently, and because it enables her to live
in Italy. She loses the radicals' permission to stay, she tells Curran,
because they say she does not "suffer and fight" (192). She appears a
rebel in rhetoric only, a parody of the committed revolutionary, and
an anti-Semite as well.

The absurd nature of the world of the novel does not refer only to
the unsavory immoral and even criminal acts presented, but also to
various situations. For example, the two sisters harboring a half of
Victor Pancev's body each recall the dictum of Solomon that the child
should be cut in half to satisfy each woman who claimed motherhood.
Further, Lina, dressed in her nightgown, throws herself into the canal,
crying out before she jumps, "Leo is the son of a Jew—I have slept
with a Jew—God, oh God!—I must cleanse myself! I die for shame!"

Leo, naked, fishes her out of the canal (156–57). Finally, persuaded by a telephone call from Robert to go to the garden of the pensione at midnight, she dances on the grave of her father, because she is told to do so by a voice coming from a boat on the canal. The absurd nature of the macabre joke underscores the general absurdity.

Thus, in *Territorial Rights* Muriel Spark presents involved contemporary problems, but she does so with a light hand. She is cynically objective, even when she presents such an evil character as Robert. One cannot completely dislike him, even though he represents the worst of human traits. "You know," Robert tells Georgio, the butcher, "I snooped. I got information. I never stole." And Georgio compliments him, "He's not a piddling pilferer. He's a born professional, this boy" (217). Thus Robert finds himself. While hiding out with Georgio and Anna, he thinks, "with a rush of pleasure: At last I'm home—I'm out of the trap." This is "the beginning of Robert's happy days, the fine fruition of his youth" (221). The actual embracing of evil puts Robert outside the pale of morality. He has become the contented evildoer, finding happiness and self-fulfillment in evil, completely outside the moral law.

The devious nature of human beings who are thus "beyond" good and evil comes forth clearly in this novel. The one sincere character, Anthea Leaver, is ineffectual, too timid to even commit herself to the pseudodetective agency in order to find her husband. She admits that her friend Grace thinks she is a "back number who doesn't know life" (164). Solacing herself with cheap novels, she loses herself in their repeated clichés.[15] She swallows what she wants to believe, never looking under the crust. And even though her husband returns to her, he still has a roving eye (which briefly rested on Lina) and one might say that the two deserve each other.

All the characters in *Territorial Rights* survive, but they do so without any growth of character or spirit. No one learns anything. All move in and out of situations, handling the present in band-aid fashion. In fact, only Robert seems to have reached some goal and will apparently end his life as a happy terrorist. *Territorial Rights* presents a very disturbing picture of a society whose members have no goal except survival in a Godless world.

Chapter Five
Manipulation of Reality

In *Loitering with Intent* and *The Takeover,* Spark continues to present contemporary life, but the former novel has more to do with the relationship between autobiography and the novel form than with characters who act out the destructive elements in society. Like her first novel, *The Comforters,* it considers the novel as an art form and depicts the novelist as one who not only manipulates reality but draws her creativity from it. The novelist, Fleur Talbot, one of the most sympathetic of all Spark's creations, may be seen to represent the author herself. In an interview before the novel was published, Sparks talked about one of her "planned novels" that was to be "in the form of an autobiography . . . called 'Loitering with Intent' which 'sort of sums up my life.' "[1]

At one point in the novel, Fleur Talbot, the novelist says, "It is not to be supposed that the stamp and feeling of a novel can be conveyed by an intellectual summary. . . . and anyhow, an attempt to save, or not save, anyone the trouble of reading it would be simply beside the point."[2] This statement might be applied to all of Spark's novels, which are difficult to summarize.

Loitering with Intent

As the novel (1981) opens, Fleur Talbot, seated on an old gravestone in a cemetery in the Kensington area of London, is writing a poem. Even though she needs a job, her morale is high. She has recently "escaped" from the Autobiographical Association where people thought her "mad," if not "evil." It is the "last day of a whole chunk" of her life (9). She is "aware of a *daemon* inside her that "rejoiced in seeing people as they were, and not only that, but more than ever as they were, and more, and more" (10–11). Using first-person narrative, Fleur relates the events that happened ten months before. At the end of the narration she comes back to the present and finishes her story.

Sir Quentin and his coterie (the Autobiographical Association) were "morally outside" her; "they were objectified." She "would write about them one day." She adds, "In fact, under one form or another, whether I have liked it or not, I have written about them ever since, the straws from which I have made my bricks" (196).[3]

The events that happened ten months before make up the central plot of the book. She had been offered, through a friend, a job with Sir Quentin Oliver to help him with the typing and editing of manuscripts being written by the members of the Autobiographical Association, of which he is the guiding hand. The ten members of the association are pathetic but distinguished, in Sir Quentin's snobbish mind, by family connections. "Only a high rank or a string of titles could bring an orgiastic quiver to his face and body" (30). The memoirs themselves, supposedly secret, have in common "nostalgia," "paranoia," and a "transparent craving on the part of the authors to appear likeable." In her task of editing, Fleur makes them "expertly worse," and everyone concerned is delighted (31). This manipulation of reality by Fleur adds excitement to the remembered incidents of the drab lives being written about, but it also begins to exert a pervasive influence on the writers. They start to believe what has been added, aided and abetted in this belief by Sir Quentin.

Fleur believes, and rightly, that Sir Quentin is using the supposedly secret autobiographies (which are not to be published for seventy years when, presumably, all involved or mentioned will be dead) for blackmail purposes. But as he is wealthy, he does not want money. His aim is to control the members of the association, manipulating them as a writer manipulates his characters. To this end, he not only advises them about their writing but also about their lives. He also provides dexadrine to help them diet and to keep them healthy.

This manipulation by Sir Quentin resembles that used by Fleur on her characters in writing her novel *Warrender Chase*. The characters in her novel enter reality as Sir Quentin and his members act them out, while Sir Quentin manipulates the actions of the members in like manner. Fleur discovers Sir Quentin's evil purpose, and when he comes to the same end as her Warrender Chase (even though her novel is finished before Sir Quentin reaches his fate), the line between fiction and reality becomes fine indeed.

Added to the above characters are Lady Edwina, Sir Quentin's Mummy, an interesting, shocking old lady who comes to love Fleur as Fleur her. A realist, she recognizes her son for the superficial snob he is and delights in shocking him with her pretense of senility. At Sir Quentin's death, she burns the manuscripts of the association, inherits his fortune, and lives to the age of ninety-six, at which time her fortune goes to her faithful manservant and her faithful companion-housekeeper, who had married in her employ and kept her happy in her last years. There are also Dottie and Leslie, her husband, who has been Fleur's lover with Dottie's acquiescence. Leslie leaves both his wife and Fleur for a homosexual lover. Dottie, called "The English Rose" by Fleur (in derision), represents the type of Catholic both Fleur and Spark detest. This gives Spark the opportunity to pit Dottie's shallowness and naiveté against Fleur's strength and courage. Beryl Tims, detestable and manipulative, trying to ingratiate herself with her employer Sir Quentin, acts as housekeeper and his mother's "prison warden and companion" (30). She speaks almost the exact words of Charlotte, a character in *Warrender Chase,* at the funeral of Sir Quentin who, like Warrender Chase, has been killed in a head-on collision.

The main action centers around Fleur's novel, which is becoming the blueprint of the life of Sir Quentin and the members of the association, and her successful attempt to thwart Sir Quentin in his evil design to control the autobiography writers. When Sir Quentin finds out that he and the others are in Fleur's novel, he has Dottie steal it. The machinations include having the publisher destroy the proofs and the original manuscript. Unbeknownst to Fleur, however, her friend Solly has sent a copy to another publisher, so all is well at the end, with Fleur's novel not only published, but with her informing her readers that subsequent works have also been published. She says, "It was a long time ago. I've been writing ever since with great care. I always hope the readers of my novels are of good quality. I wouldn't like to think of anyone cheap reading my books" (216).

Even though this appears to be a satiric comment on the ego of novelists, Fleur seems to be a thinly disguised Muriel Spark in her basic moral values, and, particularly, in her comments on the novel itself and the relationship of the novel to autobiography, or to the examination of one's life. Fleur informs the reader that "characters and situations, images and phrases that I absolutely needed for the book simply appeared as if from nowhere into my range of perception. I was a magnet for experiences that I needed. Not that I reproduced them photographically and literally. I didn't for a moment think of portraying Sir Quentin as he was. What gave me great happiness was his gift to me of the fingertips of his hands touching each other, and, nestling among the words, as he waved towards the cabinet" (17).

The mystical nature of her perceptions, the "gift" of perceiving and being able to use the perception might be likened to "grace," the supernatural gift of God given to us for our salvation, according to the catechism. This gift is pictured in the last paragraph of the novel, when, having visited Dottie in her Paris flat where they had a row on the subject of Fleur's "wriggling out of real life," Fleur encounters some small boys playing football. She remarks, "I kicked it with a chance grace, which, if I had studied the affair and tried hard, I never could have done. Away into the air it went, and landed in the small boy's waiting hands. The boy grinned. And so, having entered the fullness of my years, from there by the grace of God I go on my way rejoicing" (217). Thus Fleur lives happily, a recipient of God's grace both in her writing and in her life. She thinks happily, "How wonderful it feels to be an artist and a woman in the twentieth century" (26).

This grace manifests itself in her "good memory." She says that when she remembers things of the past, she hears them first and then sees them visually. She recreates Beryl Tims in Charlotte and Mummy in Prudence in her novel, but they appear different from the real characters. But she had *Warrender Chase* "outlined and fixed" before she even "saw Sir Quentin" (25). She had read the histories of the members of the association before she met them. Ordinarily she fixes "a fictional presence" in her mind. But here, "the histories had been presented before the physical characters had appeared" (35). She begins to consider them her own inventions.

The depression felt by the members of the association is readily apparent to Fleur when she first meets them. They are all weak people, except for Maisie Young. Fleur feels attracted to the latter, a young lame girl, who, she feels, has a "substantial" character, because "contradictions in human character are one of its most consistent notes" (41), the paradox making the character strong—which is the case with Maisie. Although insisting that there were some things in life that are not to be investigated, Maisie had allowed her own autobiography to be examined for just this purpose.

Fleur notices that Sir Quentin reveals himself as her character Warrender Chase, who was imagined by her before she ever met Sir Quentin. She recognizes the evil in his nature, having imagined it in her fictional character. She warns Dottie not to get involved with him because he is "dangerous" in his trying to put weak people "under his domination"

(63). Because of her special insights the novelist is at God's side. Fleur sees the novelist as a moral mythmaker, whose artistry lies in imagining the story mythically. She says she could have made up all the characters except Edwina who is "the only real person out of the whole collection" (105).

This confusion between characters in a novel and actual people underlies the novel. The fact that the novelist can create characters who resemble people later met in actuality is readily apparent. But Spark, through her character Fleur, goes further. The actual plot of the fiction comes true. The invisible line between the fact of Sir Quentin and the fancy of Warrender Chase is blurred when Fleur says, "Warrender Chase was killed in a car crash while everyone is assembled, waiting for him. Quentin Oliver's destiny, if he wants to enact Warrender Chase, would be the same. It was a frightening thought but at the same time external to me, as if I were watching a play I had no power to stop. . . . It was almost as if Sir Quentin was unreal and I had merely invented him, Warrender Chase being a man, a real man on whom I had partly based Sir Quentin" (181).

In recognizing Sir Quentin as Warrender Chase, Fleur recognizes also the terrible attributes of both, for like Warrender Chase, Sir Quentin is a "sado-puritan" who gathers weak people together for his own manipulative purposes and makes them feel guilty. Like Sir Quentin Chase hates women. She is sure that there was nothing for them to be ashamed of in their lives, but Sir Quentin was "pumping something artificial" into them instead of putting them into a story. If their lives had been fictionalized, it would have worked out, but what he did resulted in "falsity" (116). While Fleur, the novelist, uses real life for her novel, Sir Quentin uses the stuff of the novel for "pumping something artificial" into the lives of the members of the association. Yet ambiguity appears. Fleur did create her Warrender Chase before Sir Quentin started to imitate him.

Furiously determined to stop Sir Quentin's evil plan of manipulating lives, Fleur shows him a copy of some of his diary pages, which had been stolen for her by Edwina. These pages contain the plot that led Sir Quentin to sabotage her novel, because the plot contains the actual events that Sir Quentin is causing the members of the Autobiographical Association to work out. Fleur tells him that he must see a psychiatrist and disband the association, or she will "make a fuss." He attempts to excuse his actions by saying that he is merely emulating John Henry Cardinal Newman of whom she had spoken, in forming a circle "of

devoted spiritual followers," but she counters that he had the desire
"to take possession of people" before she ever spoke of Cardinal Newman
(190).

When she hears of Sir Quentin's death in a car crash, she says,
"Thank God he's dead. . . . The man was pure evil" (204). And
when accused by Dottie that she has "plotted and planned it all,"
Fleur agrees that she has been "loitering with intent" (215). In reality
she has been loitering, as in her mind every good artist must, gathering
sights, smells, perceptions, all to be ground into the stuff of her novels.
And God's grace, perhaps the leavening agent, insures that reality and
truth will out. Autobiography and fiction merge. As Sir Quentin was
the unknown model for the fictional Warrender Chase, Warrender Chase
was the created model for the actual Sir Quentin.

It is difficult not to conclude that for Muriel Spark, reality exists
apart from the writer's consciousness, but it is always there to supply
the material for the novelist. For her, therefore, the truth of art is based
on reality. One might conclude that the means by which the miracle
through which reality is transformed into art is accomplished is God's
grace.

Although religion does not appear specifically as an underlying theme
in this novel, there is, as always in Spark's work, the perception of
falsity in the religion of the supposedly religious, such as Dottie. When
Dottie tells Fleur that she will pray for her "to Our Lady of Fatima,"
Fleur's reply indicates her distance from Dottie: "*Your* Lady of Fatima
. . .!" (64). She is later relieved to learn that Dottie has lost her faith,
because she feels that if Dottie's faith were true, hers could not be.
She no longer has to compare Dottie's practice of the Catholic faith
with hers.

Fleur takes issue not only with Dottie's idea of religion but also
with Cardinal Newman's view expressed in a passage in the *Apologia
pro vita sua* where he describes his boyhood religious feelings and that
he "felt he was elected to eternal glory." The passage, which Maisie
Young feels is true and Fleur disputes, is: "viz. in isolating me from
the objects which surround me, in confirming me in my mistrust of
the reality of material phenomena, and making me rest in the thought
of two and two only supreme and luminously self-evident beings, myself
and my Creator" (94). Maisie insists that this idea of the two only
"supreme" and "luminously self-evident beings" goes throughout his
book. And Fleur feels a "revulsion against an awful madness" she sees
in the "mistrust of material phenomenon" and "two and two only

supreme and luminously self-evident beings, my Creator and myself."
She tells Maisie that it is a "neurotic view of life" (95–96). Fleur
adds, "For my part Father Egbert Delaney is a self-evident and luminous
being. . . . So are you, so is my lousy landlord and the same goes
for everyone I know. You can't live with an I-and-thou relationship to
God and doubt the reality of the rest of life" (96).

Her emphasis on the solipsism expressed in the passage denies, perhaps,
its underlying message. Yet, seen from Fleur's point of view (and also
from Spark's), the passage does emphasize the importance of the
individual as one of God's elect. This idea, without the qualifying
addition of humility, results in such characters as Patrick Seton, Miss
Jean Brodie, the Abbess of Crewe, as well as Sir Quentin. Even though
the religious element does not occupy a place of great importance in
the novel, it is not far away, as in all the novels, for Spark's basic
world view of a realm fallen from grace permeates them all.

Of much greater importance is the emphasis on the novelist and the
novel, and the relationship between fiction and reality. For Fleur, writing
is like "being in love and better." She says, "All day long . . . I had
my unfinished novel personified almost as a secret companion and
accomplice following me like a shadow wherever I went, whatever I
did" (60). She asks, "What is truth? I could have realized these people
with my fun and games with their life-stories, while Sir Quentin was
destroying them with his needling after frankness. When people say
that nothing happens in their lives I believe them. But you must
understand that everything happens to an artist; time is always redeemed,
nothing is lost and wonders never cease" (116). Fleur, as novelist,
creates fiction out of reality; Sir Quentin, as demon, creates reality out
of the fiction he steals from the novel *Warrender Chase*. Fleur muses,
"I thought how easy it was to steal, and I thought of Sir Quentin
stealing my book, not only the physical copies, but the very words,
phrases, ideas. Even from the brief look I had taken I could see he
had stolen a letter I had invented written for my Warrender Chase to
my character Marjorie" (145). She tells her friend Solly, "I think he's
putting my *Warrender Chase* into practice. He's trying to live out my
story" (176). And that is what he has been doing, going so far as to
encourage the depression of one of his coterie, in order to have her
commit suicide, just like one of the characters in the novel.

The writer, then, is on the side of the angels. Fleur takes reality
and, helped by God's grace, presents truth. The manipulator, the
egocentric who wishes to control the lives of others, creates fiction out

of which he or she attempts to make reality. This person is on the side of the devil. In *Loitering with Intent,* Spark shows herself to have come far from the distrust of the novel seen in *The Comforters.* As Fleur, she presents the novelist on God's side, engaged in helping Him to create a truthful world.

The Takeover

Like Sir Quentin, Hubert Mallindaine in *The Takeover* (1976) represents an inflated ego solacing itself with a bloated sense of self-importance. Unlike Sir Quentin, however, Hubert is poor and must therefore "take over" his material needs from his former friend Maggie and, to a lesser extent, from the followers of the cult he attempts to form. Hubert cultivates the myth of Diana, from whom, he convinces himself, he is descended. Whereas Sir Quentin represents the egotism of an I-thou relationship with God, Hubert expresses it with the goddess Diana.

The contemporary life of the rich with its fraudulent business practices, robberies, kidnappings, and promiscuous sexual behavior all appear without any comment by the author, presented rather as facts of life.[4] Hubert actually succeeds in cushioning his life through his thievery, and Maggie regains her fortune through engineering the kidnapping of the defrauder of her assets.

The plot, as usual, is complicated by the strands of the lives of the people who move through the novel, rather than through any momentous events. The reader learns that Hubert Mallindaine is living in one of his friend Maggie's three houses at Nemi, in Italy, a new house whose construction he had supervised and helped to furnish. He has convinced himself that the house and its furnishings really belong to him, both because he says she promised it to him and because he is descended from Diana, the ruins of whose temple are on the site. One of the other houses, a remodeled one, is occupied by Maggie's son Michael and his wife, Mary. The third is rented by Dr. Emilio Bernardini, a business lawyer who resides there with his daughter Letizia and his son Pietro, as well as his secretary-mistress, Nancy Cowan, whom he later marries.

Maggie, becoming disenchanted with supporting Hubert, attempts to get him out of her house. This is complicated by Italian laws, which favor the tenant. Hubert, sensing Maggie's changing feelings toward him, has been secretly having antique furniture and valuable paintings copied, selling the originals. He is aided in this by his secretary Pauline Thin, a Roman Catholic. Devoted to him, she does not suspect the fraud, believing that the pieces are being repaired or cleaned. Hubert, obviously homosexual, has had four young men living with him. Lauro, one of these, goes to work for Mary and Michael, where he makes love to both Mary and Maggie, as well as to the maid, whom he makes pregnant.

Maggie, feeling guilty about leaving Hubert penniless (as she believes), has Lauro put a box of gold pieces, a small fortune, into Hubert's kitchen. Lauro does so, but only after taking two-thirds of them for himself and burying them in the soil covering his mother's grave, the hiding place of previously ill-gained jewelry. While Maggie tries to evict Hubert, he forms a cult of Diana, and a friend of Emilio's, Coco Renault, tricks Maggie out of her fortune by professing to take care of her investments. The story ends with Hubert and Pauline planning to go to Rome to become in some way instrumental in the new charismatic movement. Hubert plans to do this together with two Jesuit friends, characterized throughout the novel as charlatans. He contemplates using the fortune he has put away. In the last scene, Hubert, out for a moonlight walk on the grounds, meets Maggie, dressed as a beggar. She reveals that she has just visited the kidnapped Coco, kept prisoner in one of the caves, and that her fortune will be paid back to her as ransom for Coco. She says good-night "very sweetly."[5]

Most of the characters in *The Takeover* are despicable, either selfish and uncaring or naive and masochistic. Hubert, the most evil, shows himself to be the most pagan in this story of the pagan seventies by actually reverting to worship of Diana. By virtue of his proclaimed ancestry (as a descendant of Diana), he feels that he is entitled to Maggie's bounty and the best that he can wrest from life. He "needed the best view; he had so encamped himself in his legend that Maggie had not questioned that he was entitled to the view. His secretaries from their bedrooms also had splendid views" (6–7). When he decides to talk to Maggie about installing air conditioning, he thinks that one "should not find oneself in the position of having to ask, having to wait for the opportunity to talk on practical matters with a woman of no routine." She "had no sense of chivalry. . . . [She] should have made a settlement" (18). His colossal ego rebels at the feeling that he is dependent on her; he therefore blames her for not making him independent. And her withdrawal seems abrupt to him. He blames it on her new marriage. He cannot admit to himself that there might be

some defect that Maggie has noticed in him, some reason within himself
(or in the nature of the arrangement) for her coolness about continuing
to support him.

In actuality, Maggie has "let him occupy the new house, as one
silently honouring a bad bargain; the house had been ordered to his
taste more than three years before it was ready. But . . . during those
three years and more . . . she had gradually stopped confiding in him
and even before that, perhaps, the disaffection and boredom of the
relationship had set in for Maggie" (29). Hubert, of course, cannot
recognize this. Locked completely into his own vision of himself, the
flaw in the relationship must be seen as Maggie's. And now, her change
in attitude toward him, plus the failure of some of his investments and
the departure of his young lovers have propelled him toward a crisis.

He tells Miss Thin, "I have inside me a laughter demon without
which I would die" (19). This laughter demon is his escape. It liberates
him from accepting the ordinary decent rules of behavior. If he can
escape into the myth he has fashioned for himself, that he is descended
from a goddess, he can feel himself above the common code of human
behavior. He allows himself to put a cosmetic veneer over his actions,
just as he instructs Pauline Thin to put his papers in order with no
concern for their nature, just chronological order, which, of course, serves
no purpose but looks good.

In his relationship with Maggie, he "kind of took over" her life, so
that even when away from him she felt "dependent . . . trapped."
She tells Mary, "It's really hypnotic when you get in someone's clutches"
(49–50). Hubert, therefore, exerts somewhat the same kind of spell
over Maggie as Sir Quentin over the members of his association. Both
need power: Sir Quentin to feed his ego; Hubert to feed his ego as
well as his expensive tastes.

When Hubert finds the box of gold coins next to the teapot in his
kitchen closet, he thinks, "Who . . . loves me enough to send me all
this glittering mint?" He tells Pauline that "the spirit" of his "ancestors
Caligula and Diana are responsible" (74). He cannot believe that Maggie
might be paying him off. He tells himself that it is the view from the
house that Maggie wants, not to be rid of him. He is "secure in this
lineage in which he could truly be said to have come to believe, seeing
that his capacity for belief was in any case not much. He managed
very well without sincerity and as little understood the lack of it as he
missed his tonsils and his appendix which had been extracted long
since" (96–97). The evil of his nature can be seen clearly in his inability

to recognize that he lies to himself. Like Miss Brodie, he is his world as she is hers. Each refuses to acknowledge a higher authority.

A year after the Middle East crisis of 1973, Hubert proclaims his philosophy. He was "fairly flourishing on the ensuing crisis. He had founded a church. It cultivated the worship of Diana according to its final phases when Christianity began to overcast her image with Mary the Mother of God. It was the late Diana and the early Mary that Hubert now preached, and since the oil trauma had inaugurated the Dark Ages II he had acquired a following of a rich variety and ever more full of numbers" (139). Directing his words to Pauline, Hubert preaches, "we hear on all sides about the evil effects of inflation and the disastrous state of the economy. Gross materialism, I say. The concepts of property and material possessions are the direct causes of such concepts as perjury, lying, deception and fraud. In the world of symbol and the worlds of magic, of allegory and mysticism, deceit has no meaning, lies do not exist, fraud is impossible. These concepts are impossible because the materialist standards of conduct from which they arise are non-existent. Ponder well on these words. Hail to the sacred Diana! Hail to Apollo!" (138).

By clever manipulation of language (and he approaches the Abbess of Crewe in this questionable art), the green light shows for whatever Hubert chooses to do to cement himself in a life materialistically pleasing to him. Loudly proclaiming his poverty, at the same time he periodically changes the locks on the doors to insure that Maggie cannot get in to take possession, while he systematically sells off her valuables.

Spark gives the reader an insight into the character of this master self-deceiver: "The expert self-faker usually succeeds by means of a manifest self-confidence. On the contrary, it is one of the few authentic elements in a character which is successfully fraudulent. To such an extent is this confidence exercised that it frequently over-rides with an orgulous scorn any small blatant contradictory facts which might lead a simple mind to feel a reasonable perplexity and a sharp mind to feel definite suspicion" (147). Hubert enmeshes himself deeper and deeper in self-deception.[6] He "had got into a habit of false assumptions by the imperceptible encroachment of his new cult; so ardently had he been preaching the efficacy of prayer that he now, without thinking, silently invoked the name of Diana for every desire that passed through his head, wildly believing that her will not only existed but would certainly come to pass" (145). The author adds, "in reality . . . if a miracle of good fortune occurs it is always at the moment of grace unthought-of and when everybody is looking the other way" (204).

The trickster is tricked at a garden service when Pauline, crying that she wants to "testify," reads a passage from the Bible condemning the pagan worship of Diana. Although Hubert turns this to his advantage, Nancy Cowan also testifies, clarifying the meaning of the text and declaring that Christianity desired to put an end to the cult of Diana. She attacks Hubert, tearing off his robes. Letizia joins in, and a general riot ensues. Knowing that this means the end of his credibility with the local police, Hubert, with the connivance of Massino (the lawyer who was supposed to dispossess him), cleans out the contents of the house. He knows that he must seek a safer pasture for his cult. And "his future prospects . . . seemed full of hope and drama, the two things Hubert valued most in life, all things being equal on the material side" (263).

Without much condemnation (apart from the remarks referred to above) the author presents an egotist supremely content with his life and prospering through selfish and criminal behavior. Throughout the novel there is no condemnation, even through an indication of unhappiness or reverse fortune, of any of the characters. Almost all are selfish. Maggie, self-centered and responding only to the needs of the moment, stands almost as a nonperson. It comes rather as a surprise to find that she has the acumen to take the law into her own hands, first by engaging Hubert's three former lovers to kill him (an act she regrets in time to stop them) and then by getting Lauro to arrange Coco's kidnapping in order that she might get back her fortune. Maggie and Mary both engage in extramarital affairs; Michael, Mary's husband, has a mistress, a fact known by Mary. Letizia, at the final riot, lies with naked breasts across the naked body of Merino Vesperelli, a psychiatrist, fitting scene at a pagan service.

The only good people, and they are presented sketchily if objectively, are Pauline Thin, a naive Catholic; Berto, Maggie's husband who truly loves her; Emilio Bernardini, shocked at the perfidy of his friend Coco; and Nancy Cowan, the English governess Emilio marries. On the periphery, these characters eject a bit of normalcy into what otherwise would appear as a completely degenerate, chaotic world.

Muriel Spark pictures a deteriorating world, one in which fraud is commonplace and scarcely anyone can be trusted. Even grace is absent. Pauline Thin, ineffectual, enamored of Hubert, finally prepares to leave with him. The world presented can be tolerated only by meeting threat with threat, as Maggie resorts to kidnapping, finally, to get back what is rightfully hers. Yet the horror of this world (unlike its presentation in the novel *The Godfather*) does not show forth. The comic-tragic appears in Maggie's cronelike dress when she meets Hubert after coming from the cave where Coco is imprisoned and as she sits cozily with him admitting that she knows of his theft of her belongings. Meeting illegality with illegality, Maggie tells Hubert that Coco cannot indict her. "He's too indictable himself. There are times when one can trust a crook." The "crooks," such as the Huberts, the Lauros, one's friends, cannot be trusted, and, for survival, one must meet threat with threat. In a world of lost standards, trust can no longer be taken for granted. The very cheerfulness of Spark's ending, in which the moon illuminates "the lush lakeside and, in the fields beyond, the kindly fruits of the earth" (266), attests to the serenity with which the very real horror of a pagan world is presented. The lack of horror at horror becomes the most frightening part of the contemporary, fallen world.[8]

Chapter Six
The Solution

In both *The Driver's Seat* and *The Only Problem* Spark departs from her emphasis on contemporary events to confront, in a way reminiscent of her early novels, the problem of existence. The confrontation, however, appears on a deeper level, so that while *The Driver's Seat* resembles *The Comforters* in its investigation of plot making and *The Only Problem* resembles *Memento Mori* in its exploration of suffering, the later novels probe on a deeper level. Lise in *The Driver's Seat* solves the problem of existence by orchestrating her own murder; Harvey in *The Only Problem* solves it by accepting its inherent paradox.

The Driver's Seat focuses on an attempt to make life conform to the plot of a novel.[1] The individual makes events happen according to a plan. It is similar in this way, therefore, to *Loitering with Intent* as well as to *The Comforters,* in both of which literature and reality become transposed but yet complement each other. In *The Driver's Seat,* Lise makes reality conform to her own plan, although there is a suggestion that people and events await her use of them. As she arranges reality to suit her preconceived design, she also represents the masochist, dissected to show both the motivation for masochism and the result of the aberration.

The Driver's Seat

The plot of this novel (1970) concerns Lise, thirty-four years old, who goes on a vacation from her work in an accounting office. On the plane to Italy, she selects a young man to sit next to, but on looking at her, he becomes frightened and changes his seat. Arriving at her destination, Lise searches for this young man, ignoring other men who wish to make her acquaintance, until she finally finds him at his hotel. He had been avoiding her, as he had seen her with his aunt earlier at the hotel. She persuades him to accompany her to a remote site and to kill her. This he does.

From the very beginning Lise is in the driver's seat. She sets the stage and writes the acts for the play that will end with her murder.

The novel opens with her at a dress shop, but she refuses to buy a dress because "the dress won't hold the stain."[2] She shouts at the salesperson as she leaves the shop "with a look of satisfaction at her own dominance of the situation with an undoubtable excuse, 'I won't be insulted.' " (5). From the beginning, two impulses stand out: Lise must have control, must be in "the driver's seat," and she must further the plot. An unstainable dress will not hold the blood she intends to saturate it with before long. Determined to plot her life and to live the plot, she directs all her actions to this end.

Her appearance attests to the determination that goads her. "Her lips, when she does not speak or eat, are normally pressed together like the ruled line of a balance sheet, marked straight with her old-fashioned lipstick, a final and judging mouth, a precision instrument, a detail-warden of a mouth" (6). When her supervisor gives her the afternoon off, telling her that her work can wait until she gets back, she laughs hysterically, frightening him. Of course, she knows that she will never be back. And when the office force tries to help her, she shouts, "Leave me alone! It doesn't matter." Later, when they tell her that she needs a good holiday, she replies, "I'm going to have the time of my life." And as she looks at the people she works with, her lips are "straight as a line which could cancel them all out completely" (6–7). A loner, intent on her plan, she needs no one.

The dress she buys, very gaudily colored, and the red-and-white striped coat she purchases to go over it do not form a harmonious blend, but rather clash. She wishes to be noticed. People will remember her, when it comes time for them to do so. Her entire attention focuses on the working out of her plan.

In her apartment, her "face is solemn as she lies, at first staring at the brown pinewood door as if to see beyond it." Her room is "meticulously neat . . . as clean-lined and clean . . . as if it were uninhabited" (10–12). She appears to be alienated not only from those around her, but also from herself. She does call her friend Margot, telling her that she will give Margot's car keys to the doorman. Her actions are merely reported; no reason for them is given; no emotion she might be feeling is revealed. It is as if a camera were following and recording actions and words. Spark is nowhere present. Lise's description as "neither good-looking nor bad-looking" gives the reader no inkling of her facial features. Lise looks at the two people in front of her on the baggage line at the airport, "either to discern in the half-faces visible to her someone she might possibly know, or else to

relieve, by these movements and looks, some impatience she might feel"
(17). This deliberate holding off of the reader results in there being
no clue to the motivating force behind the actions, which are reported
completely objectively.

Interspersed with an account of the actions Lise takes are facts that
will be apparent the next day when her body is found. At the airport
she speaks in a "little girl tone" and purposely holds up the couple
behind her. "And it is almost as if, satisfied that she has successfully
registered the fact of her presence at the airport among the July thousands
there, she has fulfilled a small item of a greater purpose" (19). The
reader realizes later that her trail has been carefully marked. Meeting
a woman from Johannesburg in a book stall, Lise strikes up a conversation
with her. She will be one of the witnesses in the inquiry into Lise's
death, repeating "all she remembers and all she does not remember
. . . and all the details she imagines to be true and those that are
true." The unreliability of witnesses (and all are witnesses) is clearly
emphasized. When Lise moves off, her eyes are "in the distance as if
the woman from Johannesburg had never been there" (23). Lise needs
people who can serve to identify her after she has been murdered. The
working out of the plot must be fulfilled.[3]

Authorial comment comes in only to present what will happen to
Lise, as in the following passage: "She will be found tomorrow morning
dead from multiple stab-wounds, her wrists bound with a silk scarf
and her ankles bound with a man's necktie, in the grounds of an
empty villa, in a park of the foreign city to which she is travelling on
the flight now boarding at Gate 14." As the narrative goes back to
Lise's selecting a young man "whom she appears finally to have chosen
to adhere to" (25), it swings between the two time elements—Lise on
her vacation, put into the present tense, and the aftermath of her
murder, put into the future tense. The reader, therefore, can see the
working out of this intricate action while knowing what it will result
in. The suspense, however, comes in not knowing who will be chosen
to perform the deed, or even, the reason for it. At the same time, the
reader must constantly try to make sense out of Lise's search for the
one who is her "type."

Lise selects "a rosy-faced, sturdy young man of about thirty" (25).
Another man on the plane, anxious to meet her, sits down next to
her. The young man selected, startled and frightened when he looks
at her, moves to another seat. This is crucial to the plot, for it is this
young man who is persuaded (or fated) to murder her. At this time,

when he first becomes frightened of her, it is tempting to think that it is because he senses evil in her. At his move, Lise feels "a sense of defeat. . . . She might be about to cry or protest against a pitiless frustration of her will" (29). Lise, attempting to plot her own life, her own story, her own murder, realizes that her plans are apparently not as easy to bring to fruition as contemplated. The other young man, Bill, tries very hard to make her acquaintance. A comic figure, a food addict, he plans to open a macrobiotic restaurant called "Yin-Yang-Young." Realizing that Bill is not her "type," she stares at a sick-eyed man behind her on the plane and asks Bill why everyone is afraid of her. Bill assures her that he himself is not.

Apparently Lise must do the choosing, picking someone vulnerable. The one she finally chooses has been emotionally ill and has also been in prison for the attempted murder of a woman. Of course the sick-eyed man is vulnerable in his illness, but not as much so as the one she finally chooses. "I was sure he was the right one. I've got to meet someone" (44). Later, at the hotel desk she is confused, "as if she is not quite sure where she is" (46). Symbolically she does not know where she is. She is lost in an ego trying to destroy itself through a preconceived plan. Like the author of a novel whose plot fails to resolve itself in an orderly fashion, Lise suffers the confusion of contingency.

And the author has apparently disowned her. When she marks the parks on a map of the city and puts clothes in and out of her suitcase, the author asks, "Who knows her thoughts? Who can tell?" (53).

All of Lise's actions lead to her desire to be remembered, so that the plot she makes for herself will be completely known. When she puts her hotel key on the desk preparatory to leaving, she asks for her passport "in a loud voice" so that people will notice her. She calls loudly for the doorman to get her a taxi. "So she lays her trail" (54). And the working out of the plot necessitates actors. Mrs. Fiedke, an elderly woman approaches her, suggesting that they might share a taxi, if they are going in the same direction. The woman does not seem to notice anything strange about Lise, but the reader learns that her eyesight and her hearing are not good. The normalcy of this keeps the reader between accepting events as usual and rejecting them as beyond the normal. Mrs. Fiedke's nephew will be chosen to murder Lise, although at this point the reader does not know this. The coincidence (or the fated act) of her approaching Lise allows the intricacies of the plot to advance, as it is the paper-knife Mrs. Fiedke buys that becomes the murder weapon.

Continuing to draw attention to herself when she goes for coffee with Mrs. Fiedke, Lise looks at her clothes to consider whether they are sufficiently ostentatious. She must constantly star in the drama she writes, and she must have an alert audience that will remember her.

When Mrs. Fiedke compliments Lise on her kindness to her, Lise smiles at her "with a sudden gentleness" saying, "One should always be kind . . . in case it may be the last chance" (58). This appears as an incongruity in an otherwise completely self-absorbed person. Lise's "gentleness," her "desire to be kind," comes as a shock to the reader. Thus far Lise has shown herself as a brusque, brash, loud, self-contained woman, intent on making herself conspicuous and disregarding the feelings of anyone else. She confides to Mrs. Fiedke that she is looking for a friend, indicating that she is not sure who he might be. "The torment of it. . . . not knowing exactly where and when he's going to turn up," (61) she says. And the incongruity of it all seems to be accepted placidly by Mrs. Fiedke, but, of course, she becomes part of the plot.

The kindness shown Mrs. Fiedke comes to an abrupt end when Lise leaves the old lady locked in a toilet stall in the bathroom of a department store. This appears in keeping with Lise's character, her disregard of anyone except those who will further her aim. But she does notify a woman emerging from a toilet stall that there is an old lady locked in, giving the problem to someone else. When Mrs. Fiedke, freed from the stall, meets Lise who is still shopping, she does not appear to be at all upset that Lise had deserted her. She confesses that she had fallen asleep.

And Mrs. Fiedke does not appear to be surprised at further disclosures of Lise: that Lise is looking for her "type," that one of the salesmen is "not my man at all. . . . The one I'm looking for will recognize me right away for the woman I am, have no fear of that" (69). And of course he has already recognized her and has tried to escape. There appears no indication that Lise's actions are in any way bizarre. As Lise attempts to bring her plot to its conclusion, Mrs. Fiedke appears as the foil to whom Lise speaks and who does not question Lise's odd behavior. Lise uses her, but Mrs. Fiedke allows it.

As Lise and Mrs. Fiedke shop, Lise buys the items that will later be used in her murder. Mrs. Fiedke buys a paper-knife as a gift for the nephew she is supposed to meet. Lise will later give him the knife to murder her with. Ironically, Mrs. Fiedke says that she is sure that Lise and her nephew are "meant for each other" (75). Lise confides that when she meets the one she seeks, she will not feel a presence but rather "the lack of an absence" (76). The affair, therefore, is a prearranged, preplanned event, making whole the two engaged in it. Although Lise plots her destiny, there appear clues that it is her destiny, so that while Lise controls her life at the same time she acts under the control of fate. It is similar to a simplified definition of predestination: one is fated to act in a certain way while apparently making the choice to act in that way.

Lise engages the sympathy of Mrs. Fiedke while admitting she keeps making mistakes in her search. She blames men in general. "Too much self-control, which arises from fear and timidity, that's what's wrong with them. They're cowards, most of them" (77). And Mrs. Fiedke agrees with her, ironically turning men's arguments against women's equality against them:

They are demanding equal rights with us. . . . That's why I never vote with the Liberals. Perfume, jewellery, hair down to their shoulders, and I'm not talking about the ones who were born like that. I mean, the ones that can't help it should be put on an island. It's the others I'm talking about. There was a time they would stand and open the door for you. They would take their hat off. But they want their equality today. All I say is that if God had intended them to be as good as us he wouldn't have made them different from us to the naked eye. They don't want to be all dressed alike any more. Which is only a move against us. You couldn't run an army like that, let alone the male sex. With all due respect to Mr. Fiedke, may he rest in peace, the male sex is getting out of hand. Of course, Mr. Fiedke knew his place as a man, give him his due. (77)[4]

The man Lise seeks must be the one destined for her. She meets the owner of a garage when tear gas, used to break up a street riot, forces her to seek refuge in his shop. He is attracted to her and holds her hand as if he does not wish to "let go this unforeseen, exotic, intellectual, yet clearly available treasure" (85). He insists on driving her back to her hotel, but on the way he drives to a lonely spot and tries to rape her. She tells him that she is not interested in sex, that she has something on her mind "that's got to be done" (87). She screams for help, escaping him by running from the car. When he catches up with her and promises that he will not harm her, she runs back to the car, "makes a grab for the door of the driver's seat," locks him out, and screams, "You're not my type in any case" (88). Thus she takes complete control, putting herself literally and figuratively in the driver's seat. The plot must run according to her directions. The murderer must be of her choosing and must perform to her cue. The garage owner does not meet her specifications.

While driving the garage owner's car back to the hotel where she leaves it, she stops the car to talk to a policeman directing traffic. She tells him that if he had a gun he could shoot her. Of course he notes the license number of the car after this extraordinary communication. The garage owner, Carlo, must endure six hours of grilling by the police the next afternoon, after her body has been discovered, because of her calling attention to his car.

Back at the hotel room, she goes through a curious ritual, examining the contents of her bag and the purchases she has made, finding the slippers and the gilded paper opener belonging to Mrs. Fiedke. It appears to be her last attempt to verify her existence.

She leaves her keys on the attendant's plate, saying that she will not be needing them. The parking attendant "looks explosive" when she says to him, "Go away. . . . You're not my type." He is "another of tomorrow's witnesses" (98).

Lise uses Bill, her acquaintance from the plane to help her find the scene that will be used in the climax of her scenario. When he drives her into a lonely section of a park, she tells him, "I have no time for sex" (103). She gets him to stop the car near an empty pavilion, where there are other couples. She feels sad looking into the empty café and tells Bill, "I want to go back home and feel all that lonely grief again. I miss it so much already" (105). That she misses the feeling of "lonely grief" marks her as a masochist. Happy only in feeling sad, the masochist Lise carries the sorrow to its literal conclusion—her own death. What further grief can there be than the actual relishing of grieving to death?

Lise's apparent pleasure in looking over the site impels Bill to remark that she is acting as if she is casing the place to rob a bank. She goes around to the back of the closed pavilion where the garbage will be picked up the next day and where Lise will be found "not far off, stabbed to death" (106).

And Lise remains as completely in control of the situation as she was when the garage owner tried to rape her. When Bill tries to overpower her, she throws her pocketbook into the bushes and shrieks that he has robbed her, alerting a group of nearby young people, one of whom comes to her aid. Another goes to get a policeman, while two others hold Bill. Lise calmly takes Bill's car, saying she is going to the police station. The police take Bill into custody, which is a happy circumstance for him since at the time of Lise's murder he is "safely in a police cell, equally beyond suspicion and the exercise of his diet" (108).

The climax leading to the conclusion of Lise's plot begins when she finds Mrs. Fiedke's nephew standing at the desk in the hotel and she tells him, "You're coming with me." He says " 'No.' . . . trembling." His eyes are "wide open with fear" (110). He is neatly dressed, as he was when she saw him that morning on the plane.

Although he tries to resist, telling her "I came here this morning, and when I saw you here I got away. I want to get away," he does go with her, "as if he is under arrest." She gets into the "driver's seat," waiting while he gets into the seat beside her, which necessitates his walking around the car. Then she "drives off" (111). At this point it seems as if it would have been possible for him to refuse to go with her and simply walk away. But there is a compulsion to carry out the plot, not only on Lise's part but also on his. Is it the lure of evil? Is it the recognition of a complementary nature, one that will make not only hers, but also his, complete? Or is it a recognition that there are some who will be completely ruled by others, having once surrendered to base motives and unable therefore to resist further temptation? He has already stabbed a woman who did not die of the stabbing. These questions are not answered, and it is difficult to put Lise into the class of the "demons" who roam the world doing mischief, if not evil, because the greatest evil redounds on her. "The world . . . in this novel is a version of hell, of meaningless contingency made meaningful by Lise's autonomous act of seeking her own death."[5]

The foreknowledge that Lise has of the plot can be seen in her assuring her accomplice that she has been looking for him all day and that he has wasted her time, when he tells her that he does not know her. She tells him he is her "type" and that he is Richard, also that he has been in a clinic. Of course, this information might have been revealed by Mrs. Fiedke, but there is no indication of that. He admits that he had had six years of treatment and that he was in prison two years previously. He confesses that although he stabbed a woman, he "never killed a woman." She tells him that he would like to, though, that she knew that when she saw him—that he is a sex maniac. But he replies, "Not any more" (112).

But when he tells Lise that a lot of women get killed in the park, she replies, "It's because they want to" (113).[6] At this point in the narrative the author comes in to say that the police "will reveal, bit

by bit that they know his record." They will continue to interrogate
him, even before she has been identified. They will have "secret dismay"
(114–15) when evidence seems to point to the fact that what he is
saying is true.

Then the author comes back to the pending murder. Lise tells him
exactly how he is to do it. She is going to lie down, and he must tie
her hands with her scarf. Then he must tie her ankles together with
his necktie. Then he must strike. "She points first to her throat. 'First
here,' she says. Then, pointing to a place beneath each breast, she says,
'Then here and here. Then anywhere you like.' " He protests, "I don't
want to do it. . . . I didn't mean this to happen. I planned everything
to be different. Let me go" (115–16).

But Lise is still in the driver's seat, and he does do as she directs.
After he "plunges into her . . . the knife poised high," she says, " 'Kill
me' . . . and repeats it in four languages. As the knife decends to her
throat she screams, evidently perceiving how final is finality" (117). He
stabs her exactly as she instructed him. He stares at her for a while;
then he takes off his necktie and ties her ankles together. No small
item of the plot she has designed will go unacted.

Thus Lise's plan for her life in actions leading to the execution of
her own murder comes to fruition exactly as she plotted it. The symbolic
meaning of the bizarre events hints at forces beyond the control of the
individual, a suggestion that life consists not only of doing but also of
being done to. Lise is the doer; Richard is the one done to. The idea
is a horrifying one. Forces of evil, evidenced by Richard's having already
gone to prison for stabbing a woman and Lise's accusation that he
hates women, cannot be fully eradicated. When forced into an evil
situation (and Richard appears to be almost hypnotized by Lise), the
individual cannot resist. He performs the required act, completing the
deed of which his previous attempt at murder had been only the
rehearsal.

When he runs to the car, he knows that he will be caught, and he
envisions "the sad little office where the police clank in and out and
the typewriter ticks out his unnerving statement: 'She told me to kill
her and I killed her. . . . She told me precisely what to do. I was
hoping to start a new life.' " He hears "the cold and the confiding,
the hot and the barking voices," sees "all those trappings devised to
protect them from the indecent exposure of fear and pity, pity and
fear" (117).

In addition to the idea of the doer and the done-to, there is also the theme of plot making. Lise has the plot of her murder carefully outlined in her head. She need only find the protagonist who will murder her, as she becomes the victim of the story she writes. She carefully lays the trail so that people will remember her, from the first act of buying the outlandish dress to a last act of giving the hotel porter her book, just before she leaves with Richard for the last scene of the play. In spite of frustrations and minor setbacks (and she is never frightened at the near rapes), she succeeds in having the plot come out exactly as planned.

Added to these is the theme of masochism carried to its deepest level, the actual murder of oneself. The masochist, full of self-hatred, can survive only by punishing herself. She enjoys the ultimate in self-punishment, the orchestration of her own murder. Lise is presented as a loner. Her actions are motivated by a need for self-aggrandizement through which she can compensate for feelings of inferiority; thus she announces over and over the fact that she speaks four languages. She cannot relate to another person except on a superficial level, indicated by her relationship with Mrs. Fiedke, or on a level in which she retains control.

The fact that Lise has been emotionally ill mars her characterization somewhat, for it leads one to expect aberrations not found in the ordinary person. But Spark considers the novel a tragedy, as indicated by her reference to Aristotle's dictum on the end of tragedy as "pity and fear," emotions the police are said to be protected from by office "trappings" (117). But Lise the masochist has no thought for anyone but herself and the drama she writes, directs, and stars in. She makes sure that Carlos, the garage owner, will spend a few anxious hours by allowing the policeman to get the license number of his car. And, finally, Richard will undoubtedly suffer for the rest of his life because of the act she forced upon him. The masochist, involving others in her self-punishment, brings punishment to others. It is a psychological tenet that sadism and masochism go together. Before she repeats in her four languages, "Kill me," she had told Richard, "You'll get caught, but at least you'll have the illusion of a chance to get away in the car" (116). This knowledge of what will happen to him and her mentioning of the "illusion of a chance" is the most chilling line in this horrifying story.[7]

And yet Spark's art transcends the horror of the story. The matter-of-fact way the events happen involve the reader imaginatively and intellectually, but never sensually. This great gift of proper aesthetic distancing allows the reader to enjoy the vivid action of the novel without the distraction of the emotions of horror or disgust. As Spark distances herself, she distances the reader. It is artistry of the highest order.

The Only Problem

In *The Only Problem* (1984) Spark confronts the problem implicit in the contemplation of suffering in a world under the control of a loving God.[8] She acknowledges contemporary events tacitly in the fact that Effie Gotham becomes a terrorist. But the benign nature of her terrorist activities (until a policeman is killed) precludes any analysis or conclusion about terrorism. The subject remains peripheral to the plot.

As in *The Driver's Seat,* the plot of *The Only Problem* is a simple one. Harvey Gotham, a rich man of thirty-five, has left his wife abruptly during a vacation in Italy because she stole two chocolate bars with the excuse that the "multinationals and monopolies are capitalizing on us."[9] For Harvey, this is apparently the last straw in a relationship becoming harder and harder to maintain. Harvey has taken a rude cottage on the grounds of a château in France in order to study the Book of Job. While he lives there, various "comforters" come to visit him, all for different reasons: Edward Jensen, his brother-in-law, to ask him to give alimony to Effie, and, incidentally, to get a loan for himself (a struggling actor); Ruth, Edward's wife and Effie's sister, to bring Clara, Effie's baby by her lover, Ernie Howe; Nathan Fox, a young graduate student in love with Effie, to have a holiday; Stewart Cowper, his English lawyer, to extricate him from the difficulties caused by his being the husband of Effie, who has become an international terrorist. Throughout the novel, Harvey does not lose sight of his primary object, which is to write a monograph on the Book of Job. He finishes it and sends it off to his lawyer's secretary in London to be typed.

When Edward comes to visit again at the end of the novel as he had at the beginning, he sees Ruth there, prominently pregnant by Harvey, Clara in her playpen, and Harvey's Canadian Aunt Pet, together with Harvey, all apparently content. When Edward tells Harvey that Ernie is willing that Harvey adopt Clara because he (Ernie), although her father, does not "want the daughter of a terrorist" (Effie having been killed in a terrorist activity), Harvey calls Ernie a "swine," saying he had better give her up for money than for that reason. Asked what he will do now that he has finished Job, Harvey replies, "Live another hundred and forty years. I'll have three daughters, Clara, Jemima and Eye-Paint." (179).

As usual, Spark does not condemn. Some characters appear more morally attractive than others; Harvey and Ruth appear better than Edward and Effie, although Harvey recognizes Effie's charm and does not condemn her, even when she becomes a terrorist. Harvey is presented through Edward's ambivalent eyes at the beginning of the novel. He envies Harvey at the same time as he admires him, both for his freedom and for his wealth. It is Harvey, becoming Job through emulating him (as far as he can) who appears to exemplify Spark's idea of a good person.

The verse "Surely I would speak to the Almighty, and I desire to reason with God" (Job 13:3) appears as an epigraph. Harvey, the modern-day Job, desires, through his study of the biblical Job, to reason with God, to find the answer to "the only problem," the perplexing problem of suffering. As Harvey attempts to live the life of Job by withdrawing, he comes to suffer as Job did by participating in the lives of those near him. Try as he might, Harvey cannot prevent the world in the form of his friends and associates from closing in upon him.

As Edward drives up to the rundown cottage where Harvey lives, he notices that the earth surrounding the cottage is barren, while beyond it is lush and green. It gives him a chance to contemplate his theory that "people have a natural effect on the greenery around them." He muses that Ruth, his wife, does not like Harvey and that they "had certainly built up a case against Harvey between themselves which they wouldn't have aired openly" (14). Thus the stage is set for Edward's ambivalent relationship with Harvey.

Coming to enlist Harvey's aid in providing money for Effie as well as to get a loan for himself, Edward attempts to find out why Harvey has left Effie. Harvey is relieved to discover that Edward has only come about Effie, and not some "problem that really counted" (18). For Harvey, at this point, the only problem that counts is the one he intends to solve, the problem of the Book of Job. He learns that one cannot isolate human beings, and thus he resolves the problem.

Yet the problem with Effie really does count. Harvey constantly wishes she were back. When Edward mentions that he is in a film called *The Love-Hate Relationship*, Harvey remarks that if there is anything he "can't stand," it is "a love-hate relationship. . . . The element of love . . . simply isn't worthy of the name. It boils down to hatred pure and simple in the end. Love comprises . . . a desire for the well-being and spiritual freedom of the one who is loved. There's an objective quality about love. Love-hate is obsessive; it is possessive. It can be evil in effect." He adds, "It's part of the greater problem" (21–22). Apparently Harvey recognizes that he did indeed have a love-hate relationship with Effie. Believing as he does in the evil nature of such a relationship, he left her.

Edward, like Hubert Mallindaine in *The Takeover*, expects Harvey, merely because he is rich, to give Effie a large settlement and to give him a loan. As Maggie is almost hypnotized by Hubert in *The Takeover*, Edward appears to be similarly entranced by Harvey. What came across to Edward's friends was that Edward "had Harvey more or less on his mind" (26). Edward wants something to happen so that he can get Harvey out of his mind. Harvey recognizes the devious nature of his actions and tells him, "If you want a loan why don't you ask for it" (29). But Edward, jealous of Harvey, wants the money offered to him as his due. And Harvey wants nothing more than to get back to his studies.

Harvey is "tormented" by the fact that he believes in God. He "could not face that a benevolent Creator, one whose charming and delicious light descended and spread over the world, and being powerful everywhere, could condone the unspeakable sufferings of the world; that God did permit all suffering and was therefore, by logic of his omnipotence, the actual author of it, he was at a loss how to square with the existence of God, given the premise that God is good" (22).

Contemplating Harvey, Edward notices that "anxiety, suffering were recorded in his face; that was certain. Edward wasn't sure that this was not self-induced" (29). Envious of all that Harvey is, Edward cannot give him the benefit of any doubt—even questioning whether he suffers. Edward recalls that Harvey, preoccupied with the problem of suffering, had said at one time that there could be only one answer to the problem of suffering of the innocent and guilty alike. The only "logical" answer is that each soul has made a "pact with God" before birth, the pact being that he or she will suffer while on earth. People are born forgetting this "of course" but they could be considered "pre-conscious volunteers." Edward had been very impressed by this involved sophistry. When he tells Harvey that he still cannot see the need for suffering, Harvey replies, "Oh, development involves suffering" (30). Spark's irony can be seen clearly in her devoting so many words to the gibberish explanation and so few to the logical one.

Further irony lies in the fact that Harvey puts baby clothes on his line every day and takes them in at night. He tells Edward that they keep women away, as there might be a baby (and presumably its mother) living in the house. He also jokingly tells him that if a baby might be in the house, police would not come in shooting. Ironically, the glib statement gets him into trouble with the police when Edward repeats it to them at the time Harvey is believed to be hiding his terrorist wife. The greatest irony, however, concerns the problem-solving Job himself, as Harvey, shunning all human companionship, becomes the ideal family man.

His attempt to shun human companionship does not succeed, as, like Job, comforters visit him. Harvey considers Ruth to be one of these "comforters." Although she resembles her sister Effie, she does not have Effie's fascination nor, fortunately for him, her commitment to revolution. Ruth is "thoroughly bourgeois by nature; Effie anarchistic, aristocratic" (62). Nevertheless it is the bourgeois Ruth with whom he elects to make his life. He recognizes the irony of his situation when he buys the château to which his humble cottage belongs; instead of giving up more and more material things, he buys more.

When another "comforter" Nathan comes and stays, Harvey is "aghast." He wonders why he allows it; yet he suffers him to stay. When both Ruth and Nathan indicate that they are now interested in the Book of Job, Harvey thinks that they believe him to be "such a bore" that he has "to bribe them to come and play the part of comforters" (63). Harvey does not suffer from an inflated ego, rather the contrary.

Harvey's attempt to live Job's suffering receives a further setback when he decides that he is overprotected. He has not been told about his wife's arrest for shoplifting. He asks himself, "How can you deal with the problem of suffering if everyone conspires to estrange you from suffering?" (65). He considers both Ruth and Harvey conspirators in an attempt to protect him. Thus, although he tries to remove himself from the arena of action in which real suffering might occur, particularly in connection with the criminal actions of his wife, Effie, he chafes against being kept from suffering. He wishes to suffer without cause, as Job did.

Harvey must learn two things: not only must he be able to reconcile God's relationship to suffering, but he must also learn what suffering actually consists of on a personal level. His attempt to remove himself from interpersonal relationships does not succeed, as he cannot abandon responsibility toward others. At this point he suspects that Effie has hired private detectives to spy on him, thus involving him in her troubles. He comes to feel that the Book of Job is "shockingly amoral." Job "doesn't reproach God in so many words, but he does by implication" (68). Harvey, therefore, reproaches God, because now he feels himself catapulted into trouble that will force him to leave his desired location to participate in his wife's problems.

Learning that Effie and her companions have committed armed robbery in his vicinity, he goes to the museum to look at a painting displayed there entitled *Job Visité par sa femme* (Job Visited by His Wife). He wonders about the painting's meaning and concludes that Job "doesn't mean to abandon his wife" (78). Job's wife in the painting resembles Effie in profile. Harvey now puts himself in the place of the Job he has newly interpreted and decides not to abandon his wife either.

Indeed, in imitating this "new" Job, Harvey tries to help Effie. When the police question him as to her whereabouts, he tells them he does not believe she is involved at all. And he "partly meant it" (80). He will help in any way that he can, even if it means fabrication.

Later, in a conference with reporters about the situation of Effie's criminal activities, Harvey denies that he is in the position of Job and uses the opening to give them an interpretation of the Book of Job, successfully deflecting their attention from Effie's escapades and their search for how much he knows about her crimes. The philosophical discourse to which he treats them concerns Job's question as to the cause of his suffering undeservedly. Job knew without a doubt that his suffering came from God. Harvey tells the reporters that Job's problem was "partly a lack of knowledge." He wanted "to reason with God" and he "expected God to come out like a man and state his case." Harvey adds that how the Book of Job got into the Scriptures at all is "the greatest mystery of all" (107-8).

The fallacy in Job's outlook appears in his desire (and Harvey's) that God "come out like a man" and reason. This entrapment in his own vision prevents Job (and Harvey) from ever finding the desired answer. In a discussion with his friend Stewart, Harvey admits that the *"Book of Job"* will never come clear. It doesn't matter; it's a poem" (127). Just as a poem cannot be intellectually understood but must rather be emotionally grasped, so the Book of Job cannot be intellectually argued because of the "lack of knowledge" of the arguer.

Just as it is impossible for one to arrive at the meaning of the Book of Job but must settle instead for a partial understanding, so one cannot reach an ideal realization of life itself. Harvey admits to Stewart that he would like to have the baby Clara back, not Ruth, and not Effie with Clara (as Effie would never be a mother) but Effie back, too. Stewart realizes that Harvey would be willing to have Ruth back with Clara but that he would prefer to have Effie "to make love to." Harvey answers, "That is the unattainable ideal" (126).

Life, then, can never be ideal, just as the *Book of Job* can never be completely understood. Life must always contain some element of compromise. The ideal that Harvey wants, mother figure (Ruth), child to love (Clara), lover to embrace (Effie), can never be attained. But Harvey immediately returns to a discussion of translations of Job. He admits that he only thinks of Effie when he is not thinking of Job, and says, "What can I do for her by thinking?" (129).

Yet he does think of her, and the thinking brings suffering. When Pomfret, a young Parisian inspector comes to interrogate him about Effie, the inspector remarks that Harvey has been trying to put himself "in the condition of Job" (143). And Harvey admits that the inspector is more or less right, and that the painting of Job's wife in the museum looks remarkably like his own wife.

Harvey learns about the necessity of suffering through his involvement with Effie's activities. When he sees a man in the police station being led away, he thinks he sees suffering in the man's "patience, pallor and deep anxiety." He asks himself whether it is by "recognizing how flat would be the world without the suffering of others" that we know "how desperately becalmed" would be our own lives if we did not suffer. He thinks of his interrupted work, his suffering because of his wife, Effie, and he concludes, "To study, to think, is to live and to suffer painfully" (147).

Like Job, Harvey suffers. Although not afflicted with poverty, boils, or sores, he becomes afflicted through the experiences of those close to him, particularly Effie. Even the interruption of the task he had set himself brings suffering, as he recognizes. And, like Job, he can see no blame to be assigned for the suffering. Neither he nor Ruth can blame Effie for her terrorist activities, which have brought his trouble. She could no more be blamed for them than "for an earthquake" (151). He refuses to judge her. If he had known that she was a terrorist, he would have stayed with her, to protect her. The reason he refused her money was that he thought she would come back. When Effie lies in the morgue and he must identify her, he at first denies that she is his wife, thinking that "more than ever" she looked like Job's wife (177). Then he affirms that it is his wife, Effie.

Although Harvey has not received an answer to his probing of the cause of suffering any more than Job, like Job he is rewarded for the questioning. He has accepted the mystery, and he has learned how to find contentment. When Edward arrives at his château in a final episode that is reminiscent of the first scene, he finds Ruth, Clara, and Harvey's Aunt Pet cozily living there. Harvey tells him that now that he has finished his Job studies, he will "live another 140 years" and live a long life with Clara, and the additional daughters he hopes to have. Thus Harvey, the modern Job, admits that he is "back to the Inscrutable. If the answers are valid then it is the questions that are all cock-eyed. . . . It is God who asks the questions in Job's book" (172). Harvey, having received no better answer to the "only problem" (the problem of suffering) than Job, lives contentedly, finding out, like Candide, that the answer is to cultivate one's garden.

For Spark, apparently, the answer satisfies.[10] The novel, unlike the others discussed, has an underlying seriousness and a philosophical tone. Cynicism and satire are held in abeyance. Although Harvey's characterization does not reach saintlike proportions, underlying the apparent simplicity of his life, there appears a genuine concern for others. In the previously discussed novels, Spark reflected a fallen world, unredeemable, particularly in *The Takeover* and *The Driver's Seat,* because there is no longer a norm of morality. But in *The Only Problem,* she presents a more optimistic view. Good people like Harvey and Ruth can find happiness together, and the questioning Harvey can live contented, having asked, like Job, and even if not given an answer like Job, having been rewarded for the questioning.[11]

Chapter Seven
Final Estimate

Muriel Spark's novels pose many difficulties for the general reader, particularly one who is interested in finding more than a brief interlude of pleasure while reading them. Yet the wit and humor of her language and plots bring one to a level of enjoyment seldom found in the contemporary novel. This apparent contradiction can be explained by admitting that the novels can be read on different levels. If one knows something of Spark's background and the underlying vision with which she views the world, the novels become more than a delight to read. They enter into the emotional life of the reader. The wealth of scholarship surrounding her work attests to its originality and its authenticity. She might be said to be an intellectual's novelist, as she causes thought as well as emotional response.

Her unique talent resides both in the way she writes and in the matter she chooses to write about. Satire is her main tool. She believes that "if you want to effectively speak out for an idea, the way to do it is more to ridicule. Satire is far more important, it has a more lasting effect, than a straight portrayal of what is wrong. I think that a lot of the world's problems should be ridiculed, but ridiculed properly rather than, well, wailed over."[1] And ridicule them she does with such wit and malicious humor that the reader perceives, at least for the duration of the reading, exactly what Spark wishes.

The matter she chooses to write about concerns nothing less than the plan of life itself. The search for her own identity, both as a person and as a novelist, started with her conversion to Roman Catholicism. Yet she admits that her conversion was merely the formal acceptance of what she had come to believe all along. Her writing started with poetry and articles. After her conversion, when she wrote her first novel, *The Comforters,* she found her form, but the first novels show an uncertainty, not in her vision, but in the form that vision must take in its transference to fiction. The solid foundation of faith on which its protagonist, Caroline, rests does not waver, but the uncertainty as to the fiction writer's role appears in the complex point of view. Likening novelist to God, Spark appears ambiguous about the question of the writer's God-like omniscience. Without understanding what she is attempting, the reader may become confused and impatient. But the delightful portraits, particularly of Louisa Jepp, grandmother turned smuggler, and the humor and irony both of situation and character, amuse at the same time.

Each novel is different, although all have as an underlying basis a belief that God created the world, but that it has fallen through the nonadherence of its inhabitants to basic religious truths, which for Spark reside in the commandments of God and the precepts of the Roman Catholic church. She never loses sight of this premise, although each novel presents different characters either conforming to God's plan or, at their peril (or ours), failing to conform.

Memento Mori, focusing as it does on the idea that death is the purpose for living, reveals the ideal Christian view of death both through Jean Taylor, a Catholic convert and through Henry Mortimer, a non-believer. Never sentimental in her depiction of old age, Spark reveals her innate respect for human beings, even those as old and apparently useless as the inmates of the Maude Long Ward. The supernatural element present in both *The Bachelors* and *Memento Mori* appears also in the trance of the spiritualist. The good Christian depicted in *The Comforters* and *Memento Mori* advances to the Christ-like character of Ronald Bridges in *The Bachelors,* which proposes a more explicit compliance with God's will, and an awareness of and belief in original sin, seen as necessary to salvation. *The Ballad of Peckham Rye* continues the use of supernatural elements in Satan character Dougal Douglas. The demons who plague Ronald Bridges and tempt him from the path of righteousness assume human form in the person of Douglas.

The Prime of Miss Jean Brodie marks a departure from the explicit exploration of good and evil shown in the novels mentioned above. Apparently taking a character from the category of pre–World War II single women, Spark created Miss Jean Brodie, the embodiment of the demon become God, the authoritarian egotist whose uncontrolled self-seeking destroys what might have been a force for good. This novel appears transitional between those whose subject matter emphasizes the effects of the fall from God's grace and those that focus upon contemporary problems.

The Mandelbaum Gate, The Abbess of Crewe, and *Territorial Rights* shift away from religion. The absurdity of the modern world becomes the focus of Spark's satire, and the horror of a world in which survival is uppermost appears in characters who prosper through their evil ways.

Spark remains objective, but she makes her characters attractive, through their ability in wit and language, thus underscoring the seductiveness of evil. *The Abbess of Crewe*, in particular, must be admired, even though underneath, her hypocrisy appalls.

The Takeover, also emphasizing contemporary evil, presents a more pessimistic view: of a fallen world so evil that redemption does not appear possible. The godless prosper. Threat is met with threat, illegality and immorality with illegality and immorality. *Loitering with Intent* is, however, more optimistic. The picture of the happy novelist overshadows the evil of the manipulator of lives, and God's grace again shines forth. The analogy between novelist and God as plot-makers indicates that for Spark the problem investigated in her first novel, *The Comforters,* has not yet been resolved.

The Driver's Seat, another exploration of this idea, carries the novelist-as-God to its limit. In not only writing the plot of her life but in actually forcing it to work out, Lise attempts to make herself God. In her satire, Spark indicates that a plotting of one's life without access to God's plan for that life results in destruction. As Lise can only relate to her own control of her destiny, she fails to use the power that really controls it. This leads not only to spiritual death, but in her case, to literal death. The masochist, the exact opposite of the self-loving Christian, works out the end result of masochism—her own murder.

Spark's latest novel, *The Only Problem,* builds on the optimism of *Loitering with Intent.*[2] In attempting to find the answer to the problem of the Christian whose faith includes a belief in a benign Creator but who cannot reconcile the suffering of the world with His goodness, Spark comes full circle in growth both as a novelist and as a Catholic. The virulent anger engendered by the contemplation of the evil Mrs. Hogg in *The Comforters* has gradually given way to a more balanced view in the approval of the naive Pauline Thin in *The Takeover.* And there are no explicit Catholics at all in *The Only Problem,* an indication of Spark's more comfortable acceptance of Catholicism.

To heap praise upon this already very much praised talent would be redundant. Spark's novels must be read. No amount of discussion of them, no analysis of plot and idea can take the place of experiencing the turn of a phrase, the delightful humor, the intelligent wit, and the pithy statement of truth found in these unique novels. One can only hope that Spark's works will continue to reach a wide audience, and that "the passionate few" (although there are many at present) will continue to bring their insights to an increasingly larger readership. Most of all, one hopes that readers from all over the world will continue to enjoy the novels that come from the "world of ideas" in which Spark lives.

Notes and References

Chapter One

1. As quoted by Ruth Whittaker, *The Faith and Fiction of Muriel Spark* (New York: St. Martin's Press, 1982), 19. Whittaker's publication of Spark's comments in this book are exceptionally valuable, as many of them are gleaned from heretofore unpublished material.

2. Whittaker, *Faith and Fiction,* 19.

3. The author made an attempt to obtain further information about this time in Muriel Spark's life by writing to her for information. Her reply was, "I generally don't give biographical details, not only from natural reticence, and because they touch on other peoples' lives, but also because I believe my work can be judged on its own" (letter to author, 24 October 1986). Also see n. 5 below.

4. "The Poet's House," *Critic* 19, no. 4 (February-March 1961):15. In this article Spark reveals how she determined to become a writer. She stayed briefly at the home of a famous poet (owners absent at the time) and touched all the poet's books and writing tools, hoping to "acquire" the "will to write." She says, "a number of lively prospects involving whole new ways of life were opening before me at that moment. But suddenly in the poet's house they all seemed unattractive beside the possibility of becoming a writer. . . . I was filled with a feeling of freedom and complete dedication which never left me."

5. Derek Stanford, "The Early Days of Miss Muriel Spark," *Critic* 20, no. 5 (April-May 1962):49–51. Stanford's information about Spark is particularly interesting, and I am indebted to him for it. As her close friend, he was able to follow both her career and her life. In the letter to the author referred to in n. 3, however, Spark cautions: "In the interest of accuracy I should warn you that a number of biographical pieces already written about me are altogether wrong, sometimes pure inventions, which I am sure you would not wish to perpetuate. Especially don't copy Derek Stanford."

I do not believe that any of the biographical references I have used could be considered detrimental to Spark, but as her comment is not specific, I cannot vouch for their accuracy other than to give my source.

6. Stanford, "Early Days," 51.

7. *Loitering with Intent* (London: Bodley Head, 1981), 9.

8. Stanford "Early Days," 51.

9. Ibid., 51–52.

10. Phyllis Grosskurth, "The World of Muriel Spark: Spirits or Spooks?" *Tamarack Review* 39 (Spring 1966):62. Grosskurth likens Muriel Spark to Graham Greene and François Mauriac in this regard.

11. Stanford, "Early Days," 52.

12. As quoted by Whittaker, *Faith and Fiction*, 25, from a Muriel Spark interview with Malcolm Muggeridge, "Appointments with . . . ," Granada Television, 2 June 1961. Whittaker obtained a copy of the transcript from Peter Kemp.

13. Ibid.

14. Stanford, "Early Days," 52.

15. As quoted by Whittaker, *Faith and Fiction*, 26, from Muggeridge interview.

16. Stanford, "Early Days," 52.

17. As quoted by Whittaker, *Faith and Fiction*, 26, from Muggeridge interview.

18. "My Conversion," *Twentieth Century* 152 (Autumn 1961):60–61.

19. Angela Hague, "Muriel Spark," in *Critical Survey of Long Fiction*, ed. Frank N. Magill (Englewood Cliffs, N.J.: Salem Press, 1983), 2474.

20. Malcolm Bradbury, "The Postwar English Novel," in *Possibilities: Essays on the State of the Novel* (London: Oxford University Press, 1973), 177–78.

Chapter Two

1. Frank Kermode, *Continuities* (New York: Random House, 1968), 203–4.

2. Joan Leonard, "Muriel Spark's Parables: The Religious Limits of Her Art," in *Foundations of Religious Literacy*, ed. John V. Apczynski (Chico, Calif.: Scholars' Press, 1982), 157. Leonard discusses *The Comforters* and *The Prime of Miss Jean Brodie* as parables.

3. As quoted by Frank Kermode from an interview broadcast by the BBC and condensed in his article "The House of Fiction," *Partisan Review* 30, no. 1 (Spring 1963), reprinted in *Continuities*, 208.

4. Kermode, *Continuities*, 208–9.

5. Evelyn Waugh's *Ordeal of Gilbert Pinfold*, published the same year as *The Comforters*, also makes considerable use of voices; see Ann B. Dobie and Carl Wooton, "Spark and Waugh: Similarities by Coincidence," *Midwest Quarterly* 13 (Summer 1972):423–34.

6. In a recent Woody Allen motion picture, *The Purple Rose of Cairo*, the confusion between art and reality is carried to the utmost when the characters in the picture come down from the screen into the actual life of the viewers of the picture.

7. *The Comforters* (London: Macmillan & Co., 1957), 3. Further references to this novel will be indicated in text.

8. The interpretation of this novel as reflecting lack of communication between people is argued by Peter Kemp in *Muriel Spark* (New York: Harper & Row, 1975), 18. Kemp states that what "gives the book 'real form,' its genuine unity, is that the characters are all Comforters, all isolated mentally, each inhabiting a private world of fantasy or of obsession that is remote and often inaccessible to others." This interpretation is not stressed by the present writer.

9. Ibid., 17.

10. *Robinson,* Spark's second novel, has not been included for analysis. It is not considered one of her most important works.

11. Derek Stanford, *Muriel Spark* (Fontwell, Sussex, England: Centaur Press, 1963), 128.

12. "How I Became a Novelist," *John O'Londons,* 1 December 1960, 683.

13. *Memento Mori* (Philadelphia and New York: J. B. Lippincott Co., 1959), 7. Further references to this novel will be indicated in text.

14. In his recent encyclical "Dominum et Vivificantem" (The Lord and Giver of Life), Pope John Paul II writes: "The Second Vatican Council . . . reminds us of the Holy Spirit's activity also 'outside the visible body of the Church.' The council speaks precisely of 'all people of good will in whose hearts grace works in an unseen way. For, since Christ died for all, and since the ultimate vocation of man is in fact one, and divine, we ought to believe that the Holy Spirit in a manner known only to God offers to every man the possibility of being associated with this paschal mystery.' " *Origins* 16, no. 4 (12 June 1986), 94. In this way, Henry Mortimer might be seen as a person "of good will" in whose heart "grace works in an unseen way."

15. Jennifer L. Randisi, "Muriel Spark and Satire," in *Muriel Spark: An Odd Capacity for Vision,* ed. Alan Bold (London: Vision Press; Totowa, N.J.: Barnes & Nobler, 1984), 137.

16. Harold W. Schneider, "A Writer in Her Prime: The Fiction of Muriel Spark," *Critique* 5 (Fall 1962):39.

17. Whittaker, *Faith and Fiction,* 29.

18. Kemp, *Muriel Spark,* 40.

19. Stanford, *Muriel Spark,* 126.

20. Kemp, *Muriel Spark,* 42.

21. *The Bachelors* (Philadelphia and New York: J. B. Lippincott Co., 1961), 9. Further references to this novel will be indicated in text.

22. Judy Little, *Comedy and the Woman Writer: Woolf, Spark, and Feminism* (Lincoln and London: University of Nebraska Press, 1983), 126.

23. George Greene, "A Reading of Muriel Spark," *Thought* 43 (Autumn 1968):395.

24. *The Ballad of Peckham Rye* (Philadelphia and New York: J. B. Lippincott Co., 1960), 15. Further references to this novel will be indicated in text.

25. Little, *Comedy*, 122–23.

26. Kemp, *Muriel Spark*, 50.

Chapter Three

1. This novel was first published in the *New Yorker* magazine. Spark moved to New York in 1962. The magazine gave her an office in which to work. She lived and worked in New York for ten months of the year while still maintaining her flat in London. She still publishes in the *New Yorker*. For example, her short story "The Dragon" appeared in the 12 August 1985 issue. Since the *New Yorker* does not do a "Profile" of any of its contributors, there has never been one on Spark.

2. In "The Uses and Abuses of Omniscience: Method and Meaning in Muriel Spark's *The Prime of Miss Jean Brodie*," David Lodge points out that "the film . . . though made with considerable care and well-acted, was not entirely satisfactory, precisely because it rendered *only* the literal and linear dimension of the story," relating it in a straightforward manner. He says further that it "is not merely the treatment of time that is in question here. *The Prime of Miss Jean Brodie* is a novel about education and religion, and insofar as the movie lifted itself above the purely anecdotal, it touched on only the first of these themes. . . . The religious dimension of the book was lost . . . because the film failed to incorporate the strains of religious metaphor which is woven into the texture of the novel, largely through the medium of the authorial voice." In *The Novelist at the Crossroads and Other Essays on Fiction and Criticism* (Ithaca, N.Y.: Cornell University Press, 1971), 126–27.

3. Spark's attendance at the James Gillespie School for girls provided her with background for the Marcia Blaine School. Gerry S. Laffin argues that *The Prime of Miss Jean Brodie* is a fictionalized biography of Spark herself. See "Muriel Spark's Portrait of the Artist as a Young Girl," *Renascence* 5, no. 24 (Summer 1972): 213–23.

4. There are many flashbacks and many projections into the future, which keep the reader aware of the outcome of the novel from the very beginning. This, as pointed out by Lodge, "Uses and Abuses," 126–27, militated against its being entirely satisfactory as a motion picture.

5. *The Prime of Miss Jean Brodie* (Philadelphia and New York: J. B. Lippincott Co., 1962), 186–87. Further references to this novel will be indicated in text.

6. Karl Malkoff in *Muriel Spark* (New York: Columbia University Press, 1968), 34–35, argues that Sandy is presented ambiguously. He calls her actions "suspect" and feels that she may be sexually motivated in her moral repudiation. He feels, also, that "her act remains ambiguous."

7. Lodge, "Uses and Abuses," 143.

8. Whittaker, *Faith and Fiction,* 109–10.

9. Nina Auerbach, "A World at War: One Big Miss Brodie," in *Communities of Women* (Cambridge, Mass.: Harvard University Press, 1978), 168–71.

10. Malkoff *Muriel Spark,* 35, writes, "Possibly, Sandy's 'transfiguration' is a retreat from life rather than a flight to God."

Chapter Four

1. Granville Hicks writes, "In this novel Muriel Spark emerges as an expert on the relations between Jews and Arabs; the shrines of the Holy Land, and the views of the Roman Catholic Church on divorce and remarriage." "A Hard Journey to Jordan," *Saturday Review,* 16 October 1965, 43.

2. Muriel Spark had also been in Israel at the time of the Eichmann trial.

3. "Interview with George Armstrong," *Guardian,* 30 September 1970, 8, as quoted by Whittaker, *Faith and Fiction,* 34.

4. Jean W. Ross, telephone interview with Muriel Spark, 30 June 1983. The interview, done in Rome, appears in *Contemporary Authors,* new rev. ser., ed. Linda Metzger et al. (Detroit: Gale Research Co., 1984), 12:457.

5. *The Mandelbaum Gate* (New York: Knopf, 1965), 27. Further references to this novel will be indicated in text.

6. Malkoff, *Muriel Spark,* 43.

7. Warner Berthoff, "Fortunes of the Novel: Muriel Spark and Iris Murdoch," *Massachusetts Review* 8, no. 2 (Spring 1967):313–14.

8. Sibyl Bedford, "Frontier Regions," *Spectator,* 29 October 1965, 555.

9. John Updike points out that "in her sublimely composed hauteur, the Abbess, of course, is the very opposite of Nixon, a print from his negative. We cannot believe it when her machinations go out of control. We scarcely believe in her crimes . . . she has none of the dreadful insecurity that led Nixon to turn a government's secret arm against the opposition party and to build himself palaces of privacy with public funds. The Abbess is beautiful and charismatic," unlike Nixon. Updike points out the differences between the two and remarks that "it is good to see Mrs. Spark, amused by our curious national occasion of self-betrayal and inscrutable justice, so near the top of her form." "Topnotch Witcheries," *New Yorker,* 6 January 1975, 78.

10. *The Abbess of Crewe* (New York: Viking Press, 1974), 115. Further references to this novel will be indicated in text.

11. Little, *Comedy,* 167, remarks, "In contrast to Felicity's honest if simpering banalities, the abbess is dignified by the vigorous perversities of her passions and her platforms. As she herself acknowledges, her 'passion' is English poetry, and during prayers she often recites poetry instead of the liturgy."

12. Auerbach, "A World at War," 177, points out that the "Abbess of Crewe" has . . . shed her humanity and lives in that self-created sphere. When we last see her exposed and enshrined, she eschews all kinship with natural forms and achieves the immortal status of a monumental thing." Auerbach discusses further the mythical nature of the novel.

13. *Territorial Rights* (New York: Coward, McCann & Geohegan, 1979), 81–82. Further references to this novel will be indicated in text.

14. Whittaker, *Faith and Fiction,* 81.

15. Whittaker, ibid., 149, discusses the content of the novels that Anthea reads as indicative of the boredom of her life and also as a parody of techniques of writing that Spark herself does not use. "These include an interior point of view, rhetorical questions, clichés, redundant adjectives, and euphemistic evasions of 'said'. . . . Mrs. Spark insinuates from the dreary tone of her parodies that the novelist should not attempt too much in the way of emphasizing 'significance' or 'meaning,' but rather rely on presenting words and deeds to evoke the readers' own evaluation of them."

Chapter Five

1. Victoria Glendinning, "Talk with Muriel Spark," *New York Times Book Review,* 20 May 1979, 47.

2. *Loitering with Intent,* (New York: Coward, McCann and Geohegan, 1981), 149. Further references to this novel will be indicated in text.

3. Little, *Comedy,* 177, writes, "Readers of Mrs. Spark's novels have seen these bricks many times. The bricks are more interesting than the straws. That is, Spark's other novels are more subtle and complex than this one in which Fleur claims to be giving us the central matter of an author's subsequent fiction. As though giving us the sketch last instead of first, *Loitering with Intent* hints of actions and characters found everywhere in Spark's fiction. Sir Quentin, although his regime of fasting and guilt leads one of his clients to suicide, is a less efficient . . . Dougal, and he is certainly less bold than . . . Robert Leaver. Like Jean Brodie, Sir Quentin plays Providence with the lives of others and forms a quasi-religious community around himself. Like Jean Brodie, he is 'betrayed' by a young woman who writes." But the criticism of this novel seems too harsh. Although Spark does create characters with similar traits (and these have been indicated in the text) each novel has a different focus and plot. That the underlying vision of the world in

which the action takes place is the same is not denied; it is a reinforcement of the fact that she sees life in a certain way. This is certainly not a defect.

4. Margaret Drabble, reviewing this novel in the *New York Times,* 30 October 1976, sec. 7, 16, says, "This kind of mixture has worked well before, and it works well here, at least superficially: the book presents a glittering surface. We all like gloss: we like to read of those so wealthy that they can no longer afford to insure their possessions, and we love to suffer vicariously as they attempt to foil their predators—by hiding their jewels in hot water bottles, by making false floors to false kitchens, by burying their ill-gotten gains in their mothers' well-tended graves. But, as ever, Muriel Spark raises the question: what lies beneath this dazzling game? Anything? Nothing? and, as ever, she leaves us on our own, for most of the book, to try to answer it."

Drabble feels Spark is "writing about money" and "the change that overtook the world in 1973, with the rise of Arab oil power and the fear of global recession," and that "we watch their efforts to defeat or adapt to this change, and Maggie's final dramatic recognition of it" (17). This aspect of the novel has not been treated here.

5. *The Takeover* (London: Macmillan & Co., 1976), 190. All further references to this novel will be indicated in text.

6. Hubert resembles John P. Marquand's Willis Wayde who, deceiving himself again and again, finally admits that he can no longer tell right from wrong. See Dorthea Walker, *Elements of Greek Tragedy in the Novels of John Phillips Marquand* (Ph.d. diss., St. John's University, 1962), which analyzes the disintegration of the moral character of Willis Wayde in the novel *Sincerely, Willis Wayde.*

7. In the encyclical "Dominum et Vivificantum" Pope John Paul II states: "In principle and fact, materialism radically excludes the presence and action of God, who is spirit, in the world and above all in man. Fundamentally this is because it does not accept God's existence, being a system that is essentially and systematically atheistic. This is the striking phenomenon of our time: atheism" (*Origins,* 95).

In *The Takeover* Spark presents the complete triumph of materialism, as Hubert "radically excludes the presence and action of God" both in his seeking of material goods by fraudulent means to insure his materialistic well-being and in his subversion of religion for his own selfish ends.

8. Although Little, *Comedy,* 169, writes that "no one in the novel has a serious vocation for either good or evil. There is no Dougal, no Jean Brodie," the lack of this "serious vocation for either good or evil" reminds one of the blowing "neither hot nor cold" quotation from the New Testament. It is the most devastating part of the contemporary world, which Spark presents with complete detachment. One can easily see the evil in Dougal

and Jean Brodie. But to fail to see that characters such as Hubert and Lauro are just as evil is proof, according to Spark, of the world's pagan outlook.

Chapter Six

1. One of the few adverse comments about Spark's novels is that of Patrick Cruttwell in his brief review of *The Driver's Seat*. He writes that her "literary career" reminds him "of Somerset Maugham's caustic summing up of the career of his character 'Alroy Kear' (Hugh Walpole) in *Cakes and Ale:* 'I had watched with admiration his rise in the world of letters. His career might well have served as a model for any young man (or woman) entering upon the pursuit of literature. I could think of no one among my contemporaries who had achieved so considerable a position on so little talent. This, like the wise man's daily dose of Bemax, might have gone into a heaped up tablespoon.' " "Fiction Chronicle," *Hudson Review* 5, no. 24 (Spring 1971):182.

One of the author's colleagues, however, an English professor, remarked that *The Driver's Seat* was the best novel that she had ever read, indicative of the truism that of taste there is no disputing.

2. *The Driver's Seat* (London: Macmillan & Co., 1970), 3. Further references to this novel will be indicated in text.

3. Malcolm Bradbury states that "the curious inescapability of plot is her subject, in some real sense her satisfaction." He calls it a religious novel. "Muriel Spark's Fingernails," in *Possibilities* 250.

4. Auerbach, "A World at War," 179, writes, "On the surface a rather archly whimsical inversion, Mrs. Fiedke's speech defines a hidden Sparkian world in which women are in 'the driver's seat' of a mysterious metaphysical collusion that underlies the world we see."

5. Faith Pullin, "Autonomy and Fabulation in the Fiction of Muriel Spark" in *Muriel Spark,* ed. Bold, 77.

6. This may be based on the psychological theory that nothing happens by chance. The victim engages in her/his own victimization. *The Driver's Seat* images this theory literally.

7. Velma Bourgeois Richmond writes, "*The Driver's Seat* is a chilling novel, its horror only occasionally relieved by the comic spirit which has informed so much of Spark's work. The vision of evil is not softened or mitigated. Long ago Dante definitely made clear that such an experience can lead to conversion as surely as a vision of good." Richmond discusses *The Public Image, The Driver's Seat,* and *Not to Disturb* as novels that "mirror the uncertainty, confusion, and violence that are daily becoming the ordinary characteristics of contemporary society." "The Darkening Vision of Muriel Spark," *Critique* 15 (1973): 71–72.

8. But D. J. Enright remarks, "Mrs. Spark the novelist does at times seem a mite skeptical about the goodness of God, or (which to some people

will be the same thing) about the power and efficacy of God's goodness." "Public Doctrine and Private Judging," in *Man Is an Onion: Reviews and Essays* (London: Chatto & Windus, 1972), 33. Although this essay appeared before the publication of *The Only Problem,* it addresses its theme. Yet it is hard to see that Spark anywhere appears "skeptical about the goodness of God," even a "mite." Rather, she feels human beings neglect to recognize God's power and to rely on His grace in their failure to conform to the world as He made it.

9. *The Only Problem* (New York: Coward, McCann, & Geohegan, 1984), 19. Further references to this novel will be indicated in text.

10. That Spark "describes understanding as vision, a new concept of oneself and the world which is based upon the individual's acceptance of a basic order in both" is pointed out by Ann B. Dobie. She adds that the "nature of that order will always be unknowable to man: therefore it is not necessary for him to understand it completely. To profit from his experience with the demonic forces loose in the world, it is only necessary for man to accept." "Muriel Spark's Definition of Reality," *Critique* 12 (December 1970):27.

Although Dobie wrote her critique long before the publication of *The Only Problem,* the idea is valid for all Spark's novels, but it is particularly pertinent to *The Only Problem.*

11. In a letter to author, 17 April 1986, Muriel Spark writes that *The Only Problem* "illustrates the point that we ought to argue with and about everything, including God. But the arguments of God are not rational by nature." Obviously the arguments are not "rational" because they are arguments human beings ascribe to God, not arguments of God.

Chapter Seven

1. Ross, interview with Spark, 456.

2. Spark denies that she is optimistic. In the 1986 letter to the author she writes, "I would not say that my work lends itself to the optimism-pessimism dialectic. *The Only Problem* is stoical in feeling."

Selected Bibliography

PRIMARY SOURCES

1. Novels

The Comforters. London: Macmillan & Co., 1957; New York: Macmillan Co., 1957. Reprint. Philadelphia: J. B. Lippincott Co., 1957.

Robinson. London: Macmillan & Co., 1958; Philadelphia: J. B. Lippincott Co., 1958.

Memento Mori. London: Macmillan & Co., 1959; Philadelphia and New York: J. B. Lippincott Co., 1959.

The Ballad of Peckham Rye. London: Macmillan & Co., 1960; Philadelphia and New York: J. B. Lippincott Co., 1960.

The Bachelors. London: Macmillan & Co., 1960; New York: St. Martin's Press, 1960. Reprint. Philadelphia and New York: J. B. Lippincott Co., 1961.

The Prime of Miss Jean Brodie. London: Macmillan & Co., 1961; New York: Harper & Row, 1961. Reprint. Philadelphia: J. B. Lippincott Co., 1962.

A Muriel Spark Trio. Philadelphia: J. B. Lippincott Co., 1962. Contains *The Comforters, Memento Mori,* and *The Ballad of Peckham Rye.*

The Girls of Slender Means. London: Macmillan & Co., 1963; New York: Alfred A. Knopf, 1963.

Two by Muriel Spark: The Ballad of Peckham Rye, The Bachelors. New York: Dell, 1964.

The Mandelbaum Gate. London: Macmillan & Co., 1965; New York: Alfred A. Knopf, 1965.

The Public Image. London: Macmillan & Co., 1968; New York: Alfred A. Knopf, 1968.

The Driver's Seat. London: Macmillan & Co., 1970; New York: Alfred A. Knopf, 1970.

Not to Disturb. London: Macmillan & Co., 1971; New York: Viking Press, 1971.

The Hothouse by the East River. London: Macmillan & Co., 1973; New York: Viking Press, 1973.

The Abbess of Crewe. London: Macmillan & Co., 1974. New York: Viking Press, 1974.

The Takeover. London: Macmillan & Co., 1976; New York: Viking Press, 1976.

Territorial Rights. London: Macmillan & Co., 1979; New York: Coward, McCann & Geoghegan, 1979.

Loitering with Intent. London: Bodley Head, 1981; New York: Coward, McCann, & Geoghegan, 1981.

The Only Problem. London: Bodley Head, 1984; New York: Coward, McCann, & Geoghegan, 1984.

2. Short Story Collections

The Go-Away Bird and Other Stories. London: Macmillan & Co., 1958. Reprint. Philadelphia: J. B. Lippincott & Co., 1960.

The Seraph and the Zambesi. Philadelphia: J. B. Lippincott & Co., 1960.

Voices at Play. London: Macmillan & Co., 1961. Reprint. Philadelphia: J. B. Lippincott & Co., 1962. Short stories and radio plays.

Collected Stories I. London: Macmillan & Co., 1967. Reprint. New York: Alfred A. Knopf, 1968.

The Very Fine Clock. London: Macmillan & Co., 1968; New York: Alfred A. Knopf, 1968. Drawings by Edward Gorey.

Bang-Bang-You're Dead and Other Stories. London and New York: Granada, 1982.

The Stories of Muriel Spark. New York: E. P. Dutton, 1985. Reprint. New York: New American Library, 1986.

3. Plays

Doctors of Philosophy, A Play. London: Macmillan & Co., 1963. Reprint. New York: Alfred A. Knopf, 1966.

4. Poetry

The Fanfarlo and Other Verses. Aldington, England: Hand and Flower Press, 1952.

Collected Poems I. London: Macmillan & Co., 1967. Reprint. New York: Alfred A. Knopf, 1968. Published as *Going Up to Sotheby's and Other Poems.* London: Panther Books, 1982.

5. Nonfiction

Child of Light: A Reassessment of Mary Wollstonescraft Shelley. Hadleigh, Essex, England: Tower Bridge Publications, 1951. Reprint. Philadelphia: Richard West, 1978.

Emily Brontë: Her Life and Work. London: British Book Centre, 1953. Reprint. New York: Coward-McCann, 1966. With Derek Stanford.

John Masefield. London: Nevill, 1953. Reprint. Philadelphia: West, 1973.

6. Works Edited

Tribute to Wordsworth. London: T. Brun, 1950. Reprint. Port Washington, N.Y.: Kennikat Press, 1970. Wrote introduction with Derek Stanford.

A Selection of Poems by Emily Brontë. London: Grey Walls Press, 1952. Also wrote introduction.

My Best Mary: The Letters of Mary Shelley. London: Wingate, 1953. Reprint. Folcroft, PA.: Folcroft Library Editions, 1972. With Derek Stanford.

The Letters of the Brontës: A Selection. Norman: University of Oklahoma Press, 1954. Published in England as *The Brontë Letters*. London: Nevill, 1954.

Letters of John Henry Newman. London: P. Owen, 1957. With Derek Stanford.

The Brontë Letters: Selected with an Introduction by Muriel Spark. 2nd ed. London: Macmillan & Co., 1966.

SECONDARY SOURCES

1. Bibliographies

Magill, Frank N., ed. *Magill's Bibliography of Literary Criticism*. Vol. 4. Englewood Cliffs, N.J.: Salem Press, 1979. Lists bibliography separately for each novel from *The Bachelors* to *The Prime of Miss Jean Brodie*.

Pownall, David E. *Articles on Twentieth Century Literature; An Annotated Bibliography 1954–1970*. New York: Kraus-Thomson Organization, 1978. An Expanded Cumulation of "Current Bibliography" in the *Journal Twentieth Century Literature*, vols. 1–16 (1955–70). Includes quotations from the articles annotated.

Schwartz, Narda Lacey, ed. *Articles on Women Writers: A Bibliography*. Santa Barbara, Calif., and Oxford: Clio Press, 1977. In addition to general bibliography, contains bibliographies for each novel.

Tominaga, Thomas T., and Wilma Schneidermeyer. *Iris Murdoch and Muriel Spark: A Bibliography*. Scarecrow Author Bibliographies, no. 27. Metuchen, N.J.: Scarecrow Press, 1976. A valuable, comprehensive bibliography, which includes the name of the novel or novels to which the critical article pertains. This notation is valuable because many of the articles do not include this information in the title.

2. Articles and Books

Auerbach, Nina. "A World at War: One Big Miss Brodie." In *Communities of Women*, 166–91. Cambridge, Mass: Harvard University Press, 1978. Discusses the novels' female communities, "the driving force behind men's violent history."

Bedford, Sybil. "Frontier Regions." *Spectator,* 29 October 1965, 555–56. Points out the difference between *The Comforters* and *The Mandelbaum Gate* as the uplifting effect the latter has on the reader, unlike the former.

Berthoff, Warner, "Fortunes of the Novel: Muriel Spark and Iris Murdoch." In *Massachusetts Review* 8 no. 2 (Spring 1967):301–32. Discusses similarities and differences in the writings of Spark and Murdoch.

Bradbury, Malcolm. "Muriel Spark's Fingernails." In *Possibilities; Essays on the State of the Novel,* 247–55. London: Oxford University Press, 1973. Discusses *The Driver's Seat* from the point of view of Lise's attempt to outwit contingency and calls it a "religious" novel.

————. "The Postwar English Novel." In *Possibilities; Essays on the State of the Novel,* 167–80. London: Oxford University Press, 1973. Places Muriel Spark with other postwar novelists, but calls "fictional self-parody . . . clear" in her writing.

Cruttwell, Patrick. "Fiction Chronicle." *Hudson Review* 5, no. 24 (Spring 1971):177–84. Gives an adverse critical opinion of *The Driver's Seat* and of Spark's work in general.

Dierick, J. "A Devil Figure in a Contemporary Setting: Some Aspects of Muriel Spark's *The Ballad of Peckham Rye. Revue des langues vivantes* 33 (1967):567–87. Discusses Dougal in *The Ballad of Peckham Rye* as the devil brought into a contemporary setting.

Dobie, Ann B. "Muriel Spark's Definition of Reality." *Critique* 12 (December 1970):20–27. Gives an overall view of Spark's novels, focusing on the supernatural elements.

Dobie, Ann B., and Carl Wooton. "Spark and Waugh: Similarities by Coincidence." *Midwest Quarterly* 13 (Summer 1972):423–31).

Drabble, Margaret. "The Takeover." *New York Times,* 3 October 1976, sec. 7, 16–17. Reviews *The Takeover,* focusing on the novel's use of the rich as characters and their attempt to confront the changes 1973 brought in the world economy.

Enright, D. J. "Public Doctrine and Private Judging." In *Man Is an Onion: Reviews and Essay,* 32–38. London: Chatto & Windus, 1972. Discusses *The Mandelbaum Gate* as a novel that concerns how commitment must be tempered by the private judgments of each individual.

Glendinning, Victoria. "Talk with Muriel Spark." *New York Times Book Review,* 20 May 1979, 47–48. Discusses Spark's reading and her habits of work.

Greene, George. "A Reading of Muriel Spark." *Thought* 43 (Autumn 1968):393–407. Relates her religious vision to her novels, finding that her best novels are those in which her religion fires her imagination.

Grosskurth, Phyllis. "The World of Muriel Spark: Spirits or Spooks?" *Tamarack Review* 39 (Spring 1966):62–67. Discusses Spark's use of the supernatural from *The Comforters* to *The Mandelbaum Gate.*

Hague, Angela. "Muriel Spark." In *Critical Survey of Long Fiction,* edited by Frank N. Magill, 2473–86. Englewood Cliffs, N.J.: Salem Press, 1983. Gives an overall view of Spark's novels together with a brief biography and a short bibliography of important critical works.

Hart, Francis Russell. "Ridiculous Demons." In *Muriel Spark: An Odd Capacity for Vision,* edited by Alan Bold, 23–43. London: Vision Press, 1984; Totowa, N.J.: Barnes & Noble, 1984. Discusses the power of secrecy as a theme in Spark's novels, particularly those blackmailers who live by its power.

Hicks, Granville. "A Hard Journey to Jordan." *Saturday Review,* 16 October 1965, 43–44. Reviews *The Mandelbaum Gate* and discusses the pleasures derived from reading it.

————. "Treachery and the Teacher." *Saturday Review,* 20 January 1962, 18. Discusses *The Prime of Miss Jean Brodie* as a good introduction to Spark's novels.

Kemp, Peter. *Muriel Spark.* London: Paul Elek, 1974. Reprint. New York: Harper & Row, 1975. Contains an excellent analysis of the novels from *The Comforters* to *The Hothouse by the East River.*

Kermode, Frank. *Continuities.* New York: Random House, 1968. Contains a section on Muriel Spark's novels that is particularly good for its analysis of *The Girls of Slender Means* and *The Mandelbaum Gate.*

Laffin, Gerry S. "Muriel Spark's Portrait of the Artist as a Young Girl." *Renascence* 24 (Summer 1972):213–23. Discusses the likeness of the author to both Jean Brodie and Sandy Stranger in *The Prime of Miss Jean Brodie,* calling the novel "her most public confession" both as a person and as a novelist.

Leonard, Joan. "Muriel Spark's Parables: The Religious Limits of Her Art." In *Foundations of Religious Literacy,* edited by John V. Apczynski, 153–64. Chico, Calif: Scholars' Press, 1982. Discusses Spark's novels as a link between heaven and earth, religious in their disclosure of the supernatural.

Little, Judy. *Comedy and the Woman Writer: Woolf, Spark, and Feminism.* Lincoln and London: University of Nebraska Press, 1983. Discusses the comic in Spark's novels, particularly in connection with the manifestations of liminality in them.

Lodge, David. "The Uses and Abuses of Omniscience: Method and Meaning in Muriel Spark's *The Prime of Miss Jean Brodie.*" In *The Novelist at the Crossroads and Other Essays on Fiction and Criticism,* 119–44. Ithaca, N.Y.: Cornell University Press, 1971. Analyzes *The Prime of Miss Jean Brodie* from the standpoint of its Catholicism.

Malkoff, Karl. "Demonology and Dualism: The Supernatural in Isaac Singer and Muriel Spark." In *Critical Views of Isaac Bashevis Singer,* 149–67. New York: New York University Press, 1969. Gives similarities and differences in how the two authors deal with the supernatural.

————. *Muriel Spark.* New York: Columbia University Press, 1968. This is one of the Columbia University critical studies of English, Continental, and other writers whose works are of contemporary artistic and intellectual significance. It gives a brief overall view of Spark's novels.

Massie, Alan. "Calvinism and Catholicism in Muriel Spark." In *Muriel Spark: An Odd Capacity for Vision,* edited by Alan Bold, 94–107. London: Vision Press, 1984; Totowa, N.J.: Barnes & Noble, 1984. Discusses the relationship of the novels to both Calvinism, her heritage, and Catholicism, her choice, finding that the Catholic church stands as "the one bulwark" against the excesses of the modern world.

Menzies, Janet. "Muriel Spark: Critic into Novelist." In *Muriel Spark: An Odd Capacity for Vision,* edited by Alan Bold, 11–31. London: Vision Press, 1984; Totowa, N.J.: Barnes & Noble, 1984. Discusses the relationship of Muriel Spark as critic to her work as novelist.

Metzger, Linda. "Muriel Spark." In *Contemporary Authors.* New rev. ser., Vol. 12, 450–57. Detroit: Gale Research Co., 1984. Gives biographical data and some criticism of novels. Particularly valuable for up-to-date overview of Spark's work and for telephone interview with Spark in Rome 30 June 1983.

Potter, Nancy. "Muriel Spark: Transformer of the Commonplace." *Renascence* 17 (Spring 1965):115–20. Points out Spark's tendency to transfigure the "apparently unspectacular into a parable of good and evil," and indicates that the novels should be "studied for theme and pattern."

Pullin, Faith. "Autonomy and Fabulation in the Fiction of Muriel Spark." In *Muriel Spark: An Odd Capacity for Vision,* edited by Alan Bold, 71–93. London: Vision Press, 1984; Totowa, N.J.: Barnes & Noble, 1984. Discusses the ambiguity in Spark's novels, particularly *The Driver's Seat* and *The Prime of Miss Jean Brodie,* indicating that it is not the task of the novelist "to explain ambiguity, merely to define it."

Randisi, Jennifer L. "Muriel Spark and Satire." In *Muriel Spark: An Odd Capacity for Vision,* edited by Alan Bold, 132–47. London: Vision Press, 1984; Totowa, N.J.: Barnes & Noble, 1984. Discusses Spark's satiric vision, calling blackmail, which appears in many of her novels, "the great social leveler."

Richmond, Velma Bourgeois. "The Darkening Vision of Muriel Spark." *Critique* 15 (1973):71–85. Gives particularly good interpretations of *The Driver's Seat, The Public Image,* and *Not to Disturb.*

Schneider, Harold W. "A Writer in Her Prime: The Fiction of Muriel Spark." *Critique* 5 (Fall 1962):36–45. Gives a critique of Spark's early novels, calling her "a very good writer."

Stanford, Derek. "The Early Days of Miss Muriel Spark." *Critic* 20, no. 5 (April-May 1962):49–51. Gives interesting and valuable information about her life and her career, from one who joined in critical writing with her.

————. *Muriel Spark.* Fontwell, Sussex, England: Centaur Press, 1963. By a friend of Spark's; particularly good for its recollections of her early days as a novelist and her early novels. Regarding Stanford's references, see Note 5, Chapter 1.

Updike, John. "Topnotch Witcheries." *New Yorker,* 6 January 1975, 76–81. Discusses "Watergate" as Spark's inspiration for *The Abbess of Crewe* and points out the differences in the abbess's characterization and Nixon's personality.

Whittaker, Ruth. *The Faith and Fiction of Muriel Spark.* New York: St. Martin's Press, 1982. An excellent scholarly study of Muriel Spark's novels, containing a wealth of reference and critical material on the author.

Index